SEEK THE EXPANSION OF

GOD'S KINGDOM

By

Asewie Kennedy,

August, 2013

Unless otherwise stated, all scripture quotations
are taken from the **King James Version** of the
Bible

ISBN: 9964-92-508-5

_Email: asennedy@hotmail.com/
evangelistasewiekennedy@gmail.com._

Contact:
+233 (0) 549011337

_Printed and Published by GILLBT
Printing Press, Tamale,
P.O. Box TL, 378
Tel:+233(0)242210791_

TABLE OF CONTENT

iv

Preface

The greatest evangelist of the 20th century, **Evangelist Billy Graham**, speaking at the Amsterdam Conference for Itinerant Evangelists, said: **"One of the greatest needs today is for the Church throughout the world to recognize and recover the legitimacy and importance of the gift of the Evangelist."** Perhaps it is because the world church is not sure what evangelism is.

Our English word *"evangelism"* (*"evangelize,"* *"evangelist"*) comes from the Greek word, *euangelion* — meaning *"good news"* or the *"Gospel."* In its basic meaning, evangelism (*euangelidzō*) is the preaching of the Gospel. It is the fulfillment of Christ's Great Commission to His churches (Mark 16:15).

v

Foreword

What constitute a great Christians experience, and how is a great Christian's experience or story told?

In telling the story of one's Christians experience this little book answers these questions. The story told here is the author's personal Christian experience as a student who was involved in campus evangelism and soul winning. He dilates a little on the moral lifestyle of much of our so called Christian workers, especially of those involved in the pastoral ministry.

Ken's involvement in campus evangelism made him understand well the issues he speaks about in this book. **Asewie Kennedy** provides the reader with vivid insight into the issues he discusses. He gives us all a chance to learn from the experience he had gathered over the years. This book is warmly recommended as a must read for all.

Rev. Bernard Asewie
Head Pastor: Evangelical Church of Ghana
(Wurishie Assembly, Tamale)

Acknowledgement

When Allan Wells of Scotland won the 100 meter
dash at the 1980 Olympics in Moscow, he said,
"That's for Eric Liddell." In so doing he acknowledged the inspiration and influence Liddell had
been to him and to all Scotsmen since the 1924
Olympics in Paris. That's when Liddell opted out
of a great chance at winning the prestigious 100
meter championship because the day of the race
conflicted with His Christian convictions, only to
set an Olympic record in winning the gold medal
on another day in the 400 meters.

As Allan Wells acknowledged the influence of
someone who had died almost forty years before
him, so I want to acknowledge the influence of
men I have never met except through their writ-

ings and biographies and preaching tapes. But they are men whose thoughts and lives have profoundly changed mine. They are spiritual giants on whose shoulders I stand today.

First of all I gives thanks to God for his grace and strength throughout this process. Thanks to Rev. Bernard Asewie, and Papa Dag Heward-Mills. My life and ministry are immeasurably better because of theirs.

I also want to show my gratitude to these in my own day who have enriched my life in ways that have had a direct bearing on this book. Thanks to Mr. David Appiah of ARK CHEMIST Tamale, for his willingness to help a young passionate Christian he hadn't met before. Thanks to Brothers; Mac-Dabara Daniel, Christian Mimshack Kwesi, Martey Raymond and Karim Shem for their friendship, motivation, encouragement and for challenging me to think extra.

Thanks to Pastor Edem Forster of (Fountain Gate Chapel, Philadelphia Pastures Tamale) for his genuine, unselfish excitement about this book and for being such a joy to help me to publish this book.

Thanks to Sister Nancy for her help in entering data and for assisting with so many details and information.

Thanks to Brother Abraham Muniru for his genuine friendship and encouragement without which this book probably would not have been written and published.

Thanks to Brother Shadrach Bavor of (Zenith Bank Tamale) and Dr. Joseph Sonlaari of (Tamale Teaching Hospital) for being such an affirming encouragers and motivators from beginning to end.

Thanks to all friends and love ones who have been praying for me and for supporting me with extra love throughout the process of writing this book. Thanks to GILLBT Press and Staff who patiently endured so much that this book might be published.

Dedication

This book is dedicated to my Dad, Rev. Bernard Asewie for always being there to provide all the backing I needed in my spiritual and Christian growth... Thanks for being a mentor and an inspiration to me.

To my spiritual father Evangelist Dag Heward-Mills, though the Elijah's and the Jeremiah's are not there today to take up their mantels but you have made yourself available so I could tap into your gifts of writing, teaching and healing. Thank you for being a source of encouragement and inspiration to me, God bless you and increase your ministry into another dimension

The Book

Many Christians are struggling and panicking when the issue of evangelism is been raised in and outside the church, some claim to be ashamed to evangelize which is often the primary excuse, but one needs to know that we have been commission to go evangelize the entire planet. In this book, Asewie Kennedy teaches with practical examples on how evangelism can be made very effective and how important the good news of Jesus Christ needs to be sent out to the unreached. Enjoy this great book by Asewie Kennedy.

Introduction

THE WORK OF AN EVANGELIST

Timothy was instructed to **"do the work of an evangelist"** (II Timothy 4:5). This work is exemplified in the ministry of Philip — the only man in the Bible who is directly called an evangelist (Acts 21:8).

Philip's ministry involved three things: preaching the Gospel (Acts 8:5, 35), baptizing those who believed (Acts 8:12, 38), and organizing churches (Acts 8:14). Therefore, New Testament evangelism is church-planting and an evangelist is what most people would call a **"missionary."**

The sending of two pastors from the *"mother"* church in Jerusalem to Samaria demonstrates that

2

Philip was not a freelancing evangelist. He remained (and evangelized) under the authority of the church he once served as a deacon (Acts 6:5).

The ministry of evangelism is itinerant (Acts 8:40). As churches are organized, evangelists move on to start other churches. Philip evidently planted several churches along the coastal plains of Israel, including those at Lydda (Acts 9:32) and Joppa (Acts 9:38), before settling down in Cæsarea.

The call of an Evangelist
According to Ephesians 4:11, evangelists (like pastors) are a gift to the Lord's churches from Jesus Christ. This means first of all that they are recipients of a divine call into the ministry (I Timothy 1:12) and, secondly, that God raises them up in the churches and equips them to spearhead a church's fulfillment of the Great Commission.

The example of Acts 13:1-2 shows that pastors can be separated for evangelistic ministry (and later return to the pastorate when they have

3

completed their mission, Acts 14:28; 15:35). Apparently the office of a bishop and the work of an evangelist were much more fluid than is commonly practiced today.

The Training of an Evangelist

Just as there is a natural law of physical reproduction (Genesis 1), there is a law of *spiritual* reproduction (**"Christians produce Christians; Churches produce Churches; and Preachers produce Preachers"**). God-called men are prepared for the ministry in the manner set forth by II Timothy 2:2.

This scriptural pattern is exemplified by the church at Ephesus, a church that was planted by Paul and his team (Acts 19). Almost a year after he left that city, Paul met in Miletus with the church's pastors and reminded them in his parting charge that he had spent three years **"night and day"** teaching and training them (Acts 20:31). During that time, two things were accomplished: first, God-called men were trained as elders or pastors (Acts 20:17) to shepherd the church; second, God-called men must have been

4

trained and sent out by the church as evangelists — because *"all Asia heard the Gospel"* (Acts 19:10). One of such man was Epaphras, who labored at Colosse (Colossians 1:7).

The methods of Evangelism
There are two key passages that deal with methodology.

New Testament evangelism was first instituted by the Lord Jesus Christ — a year-and-a-half *before* He left His church with the Great Commission. It is recorded in Luke chapters 9 and 10. The account of the sending of the seventy in Luke 10:1-17 yields several principles of evangelism that are mirrored in the evangelistic activities of the church at Antioch in Acts 13&c.

For example:

EVANGELISM IS	LUKE 10	
Church Centered It is not a man-centered ministry.	This event is set in the context of the church that was founded by Jesus Christ during His earthly ministry (Luke 6:13; I Corinthians 12:28)	
Church Sent No mission boards, clearing-houses, or man- made sending agencies are found in the Word of God.		
Divinely Appointed The Lord selects men out of the church for the work.	"After these things the LORD APPOINTED other seventy also" (verse 1)	
Team Ministry Evangelists work in teams of two or more.	"And sent them TWO AND TWO" (verse 1)	
Spirit Led Evangelists depend on the Spirit's leading as to where and when they preach.		
Itinerant Evangelists take the Gospel everywhere, rather than to a fixed place. Paul was an international evangelist.	"into EVERY city and place" (verse 1)	
Vulnerable Evangelists serve on the "front lines" of a spiritual war.	"Go your ways: behold, I send you forth as lambs among wolves" (verse 3)	

	ACTS 13.
	"Now there were in the CHURCH that was at Antioch" (13:1)
	"And when they had fasted and prayed, and laid their hands on them, they SENT them away" (13:3).
	"the HOLY GHOST said, SEPARATE me Barnabas and Saul for the work whereunto I have called them" (13:2)
	"Barnabas AND Saul ... and they had also John to their minister" (13:2,5)
	"Being sent forth by the Holy Ghost" (13:4) See: Acts 8:39; 10:19-20; 11:12; 16:6-7.
	Salamis (13:5) Paphos (13:6) Perga (13:13) — twice Pisidian Antioch (13:14) — twice Iconium (13:51) — twice Lystra (14:6) — twice Derbe (14:6)
	"Elymas the sorcerer ... withstood them, seeking to turn away the deputy from the faith" (13:8) "When the Jews saw the multitudes, they were filled with envy, and spake against those things which were spoken by Paul, contradicting and blaspheming" (13:45) "There came thither certain Jews from Antioch and Iconium, who persuaded the people, and, having stoned Paul, drew him out of the city, supposing he had been dead" (14:19)

Faith Dependent Evangelists depend upon the giving of God's people. They are NOT mendicant NOT mendicant	"Carry neither purse, nor scrip, nor shoes" (verse 4) "And in the same house remain, eating and drinking such things as they give: for the laborer is worthy of his hire. And into whatsoever city ye enter, and they receive you, eat such things as are set before you" (verses 7-8)
Benevolent Evangelists may meet the physical needs of people as an avenue to the spiritual.	"And heal the sick that are therein" (verse 9)
Purposeful Evangelists preach the Gospel.	"Say unto them, The kingdom of God is come nigh unto you" (verse 9) "Be ye sure of this, that the kingdom of God is come nigh unto you" (verse 11).
Limited A church's responsibility is to preach the Gospel to every creature — not to win every soul to Christ. When evangelists have faithfully fulfilled their responsibility, they must move on. See: Matthew 16:19.	"Into whatsoever city ye enter, and they receive you not, go your ways out into the streets of the same, and say, Even the very dust of your city, which cleaveth on us, we do wipe off against you" (verses 10-11)

crip,	Paul was willing to work with his hands (Acts 18:3; 20:34) Paul was dependent upon the sacrificial giving of God's people (Philippians 4:11-18; I Corinthians9:4-14) As team leader, Paul was responsible for the welfare of his fellow workers(Acts 20:34d)
	The exercise of the *temporary+ "sign gifts" was to authenticate and confirm the Gospel message that was preached (Mark 16:17 -18, 20).
od is	"they PREACHED the word of God" (13:5) "Be it known unto you therefore, men and brethren, that through this man is PREACHED unto you the forgiveness of sins: And by him all that believe are justified from all things, from which ye could not be justified by the law of Moses" (13:38-39) "And there they PREACHED the Gospel" (14:7) "And when they had PREACHED the gospel to that city" (14:21)
	"It was NECESSARY that the word of God should first have been spoken to you … lo, we turn to the Gentiles" (13:46)

Eternal When people reject the Gospel, they only condemn themselves.	"But I say unto you, that it shall be more tolerable in that day for Sodom, than for that city. Woe unto thee Chorazin! Woe unto thee, Bethsaida! For if the mighty works had been done in Tyre and Sidon, which have been done in you, they had a great while ago repented, sitting in sackcloth and ashes. But it shall be more tolerable for Tyre and Sidon at the judgment, than for you. And thou, Capernaum, which art exalted to heaven, shalt be thrust down to HELL." (verses 12-15)	
Fruitful See: Psalm 126:5-6.	"And the seventy RETURNED again with joy" (verse 17)	

The challenge for 21st Century Evangelism

Evangelism has long been an "Achilles heel" for Bible-believing Churches. Godly men, with a sincere and zealous desire to see precious souls saved and the cause of Christ advanced throughout the world, have devised well-meaning methods that have not only moved

shall	
ne in	"but seeing ye put it from you, and judge yourselves unworthy of everlasting life" (13:46)
. But	
own	
	"And thence sailed to Antioch, from whence they had been recommended to the grace of God for the work which they fulfilled. And when they were come, and had gathered the church together, they rehearsed all that God had done with them, and how he had opened the door of faith unto the Gentiles" (14:26-27)

away from established New Testament principles, but have created the seeds of destruction and apostasy. For example, in 1814, the seeds of demise were planted when well-intentioned

Baptists formed the American Baptist Missionary Union to sponsor Adoniram Judson's ministry in Burma. This move led directly to conventionism and the "Cooperative Program." Even to this day, many Baptist groups almost instinctively feel a need to organize some kind of mission-sending agency. While they vociferously claim to be independent, history is not on their side.

It's not a question of whether man's methods will work. They do! Anytime the Gospel of Jesus Christ is proclaimed it will have its intended effect (Isaiah 55:11; Romans 1:16; Hebrews 4:12). The real question is, "Can God's way be improved upon?"

Here is the challenge:
Why not allow the Lord to direct His CHURCH to seek a vision for the "regions beyond?" The church at Antioch and its pastors did!

Why not allow the Lord to raise up men from within a church to fulfill that vision? The church at Antioch did!

Why not train God-called men within a church, rather than sending them off to an institution where others will teach them?

Why not practice team ministry? The Lord Jesus Christ did. The Church at Antioch did. Peter and Paul did. Employ the Ecclesiastes 4:9-10 principle.

Why not send evangelists out directly from the Church? The church at Antioch did. A church is able to do all that a "mission office" can do ... and more!

Why not see evangelists as being responsible and accountable to their sending, sponsoring, and supporting church?

Why not send evangelists to a People rather than a place? Paul was an apostle to the gentiles; Peter to the Jews.

Why not allow evangelists the liberty to follow the SPIRIT'S leading as to where they should go and how they should labor?

Why not view failure as success? An Itinerant ministry seeks people who will listen, and moves on when they won't.

Why not allow Pastors to do the work of an evangelist by practicing team ministry IN the Church as well as through its outreach? The church at Antioch did.

Evangelism is to be the heart and soul of every Bible-believing Church. The parting commandment of the Lord Jesus Christ is reiterated five times in the Gospels and the book of Acts (Matthew 28:18-20; Mark 16:15; Luke 24:47; John 20:21; Acts 1:8), and in the last gracious invitation of the Word of God (Revelation 22:17). It is that important!

Evangelism is not a question of "IF," but of "HOW?" We all acknowledge the Commission; may we also see that the Master has also given us the "how" in the principles and practice of the New Testament churches. I pray that as you read this book you will have the insight and your spirit will be stirred up to go evangelize, because it is a mandate give to us by our Lord Jesus Christ. God bless you as you read this book.

Chapter One

THE GREAT COMMISSION A PERSONAL INSTRUCTION

The Great Commission is one of the most significant and important passages in the Bible. First, it's the last recorded personal instruction given by Jesus to His disciples. Second, it's a special calling from Jesus Christ to all His followers to take specific actions while on earth. This Great commission can be seen in the book Matthew: *"Then Jesus came to them and said, 'All authority in heaven and on earth has been given to me. Therefore go and make disciples of all nations, baptizing them in the name of the Father and of the Son and of the Holy Spirit, and*

15

teaching them to obey everything I have com-
manded you. And surely I am with you always,
to the very end of the age'" (Matthew 28:18-20).

The Great Commission is the end of a Gospel and the beginning of faith in action for all Christians. This command from Jesus is significant because it's a personal instruction for Christians to have a profound faith in Jesus Christ as indicated in verse 18. *"All authority in heaven and on earth has been given to me."* This is an incredibly a powerful statement which demands faith in Jesus Christ, validating His power and authority in the lives of Christians and their commitment to Him. This verse acts as a clear claim to Christ's omnipotence, and therefore His deity. If Christians do not believe this statement, complete faith does not exist. Jesus is very clear about His authority in the world it is complete and total from the beginning of time itself (John1:1-3).In Matthew 28:19, Jesus gives His believers specific directions to follow after they have affirmed their faith. *"Go therefore and make disciples of all the nations, baptizing them in the name of the Father and of the Son and of the Holy Spirit."* Jesus calls all His followers to act and share the Good News of salvation throughout the world. People hear this calling and travel each year on missionary trips throughout the earth, spreading the word of Jesus Christ. Many Christians have made incredible sacrifices, traveling to remote regions of the world beyond the civilized cities into jungles and deserts. Mission fields can also be very close to home. It could be a neighbor who has not heard the Good News, or a poverty stricken area just down the road where people can't afford Bibles. In this 21st century we live in, the **Internet** has become a mission field where people can reach out and share Christ's love. The places and people who need to hear the Gospel are everywhere! Another important aspect of verse 19 is that Christ is specifically teaching the doctrine of the Trinity to His followers. The three Persons of the Godhead are each equally and fully God and here presented in the logical order of Father, Son and Holy Spirit - yet only One God from the beginning (see Romans 1:20).Finally, in verse 20, Jesus provides specific direction with affirmation to His followers, *"teaching them to observe all things that I have commanded you;*

17

and lo, I am with you always, even to the end of the age." Christians are instructed to teach others about Jesus Christ and the entirety of His truth. We can't profess Christ as Savior and Lord, while rejecting some of His teachings. As we teach Christ's truths, verse 20 declares that we can be confident, in faith, that Jesus Christ will support us. This fact has proven trustworthy throughout the centuries as millions of believers have heard, accepted and shared the Good News of Jesus Christ. Yes, Christ has ascended back to heaven, but He is present by the power of the Holy Spirit in every believer!

The Great Commission is a personal Calling

In the Great Commission, Jesus calls every Christian to step out in faith and spread the Good News. This is faith in action! People who obey this command change their spiritual lives forever! It could be spreading the Good News to a neighbor or moving to another country to reach out the people. It could be sharing with less fortunate kids down the street or spreading the Word in a town two hours away from where you live. Wherever we go, every faithful Christian is compelled through obedience to share the Gospel. If you're a believer in Jesus Christ, where has He called you to go? Who has God put on your heart to share the gift of salvation? What small or large steps can you take, with the knowledge that Christ will be by your side, *"to make disciples of all the nations"*? Today, many people have heard the gospel of grace, which is good. Many preachers preach it, but they also proclaim that if you only believe and confess Jesus as your personal savior, you will get into heaven and you will have eternal security and eternal life. Many churches seldom teach about repentance. When I inquired about this, the answer I got from them was that repentance after conversion was a separate deal from the salvation package, that it is about Christian living, and that some *"experts"* (i.e. revivalist) can preach about that if they got a special calling. (There are but a few revivalists in the last hundreds of years)But the Bible clearly teaches that if we don't repent, we are not saved. Repentance isn't just a onetime act or experience. It is necessary to repent whenever one commits sins. Otherwise, one will live in sin and risk dying in it. What happens if we die in sin? We won't go to heaven. Let me |explain. Repentance is one of the Initial Conditions to Salvation *"from that time Jesus began to preach, and to say, Repent: for the kingdom of heaven is at hand"*. Matthew 4:17.

"Tell you, no! But unless you repent, you too will all perish". Luke 13:3.

"Now after that John was put in prison, Jesus came into Galilee, preaching the gospel of the kingdom of God, and saying, the time is fulfilled, and the kingdom of God is at hand: repent ye, and believe the gospel". [Repent, and then believe. Not vice versa] Mark 1:14-15

When Jesus began to preach, he didn't ask people to confess and believe in the gospel and then repent, but he first asked people to repent. Repentance is the first thing that Jesus asks us to do. If we don't repent, which is the first thing Jesus asked for, then how can we receive the rest of the "salvation package"?

Later, Jesus revealed other truth to his disciples, but the first step was to repent. *"Then Peter said unto them, Repent, and be baptized every one of you in the name of Jesus Christ for the remission of sins, and ye shall receive the gift of the Holy Ghost"* Acts 2:38

"Repent, then, and turn to God, so that your sins may be wiped out, that times of refreshing may come from the Lord", Acts 3:19.

"But shewed first unto them of Damascus, and at Jerusalem, and throughout all the coasts of Judaea, and then to the Gentiles, that they should repent and turn to God, and do works meet for repentance." Acts 26:20.

After Jesus ascended to heaven, the disciples received the Holy Spirit, and they too began to preach. The requirement to repent didn't change. They still asked people to repent before anything else after the Cross and Ascension.

No repentance no forgiveness and no forgiveness no salvation. We Should Repent Of Our Past,

Present; And Future Sin Whenever God Convicts Us Repentance is as needed. Anytime the Holy Spirit convicts you of a particular sin (John 16:7-8), you have to repent and confess it right there and then, no matter how long ago you have committed it before. (1 John 1:8-9)Refusal and negligence to do so would be quenching or grieving the Holy Spirit. (1 Thess 5:19; Eph 4:3)

This doesn't have to be a passive process. If we want to maintain an intimate relationship with God, we have to seek God's guidance on this actively. In time, we will become closer to God and sin much less. Some teachers might tell you that God has forgiven us of our past, present, and future sin at the point of time when we become a Christian. That is another lie from the devil, that is very misleading— a big but subtle error.

The redemption of Jesus Christ is effective for the past, present, and future, but it is not automatic and once-and-for-all experience. We can still reject His redemption anytime if we choose to give up our belief in the pure Gospel, or still stay glued to certain sins we do not want to repent from. Some teachers also tell you that salvation of the Old Testament is different than the New Testament. In fact, in both Testaments, the saints receive salvation through faith, in Christ. Nothing that we do is good enough for us to earn our salvation, whether a believer is from the Old Testament era or the New Testament era.

See how King David from the Old Testament era deals with his sins from the psalms below: *"Who can understand his errors? Cleanse thou me from secret faults. [David confesses and asks for forgiveness even for hidden sins that he isn't aware of]Keep back thy servant also from presumptuous sins [willful and prolonged sins]; let them not have dominion over me: then shall I be upright, and I shall be innocent from the great transgression"*. Psalm 19:12-13.

David prays for divine interventions and protections to keep him from future sins, while he trust God to blot out his past, hidden sins that he couldn't even remember and those he is not aware of.

"Search me, O God, and know my heart: try me, and know my thoughts: And see if there be any wicked way in me, and lead me in the way everlasting". Psalm 139:23-24.

David is always careful. He is watchful and alert. He never stop asking God to convict him of any leftover sin or secret sin that are outside of his limited awareness so he can stay on the narrow path to heaven. (Matthew 7:14).

Sometime, David goes through heavy convictions. Maybe God is doing a major spiritual surgery on him — He is bringing many hidden sins to light:

"For innumerable evils have compassed me about: mine iniquities have taken hold upon me, so that I am not able to look up; they are more than the hairs of mine head: therefore my heart faileth me. Be pleased, O LORD, to deliver me: O LORD, make haste to help me." Psalm 40:12-13

The heavy conviction of sins is a spiritual crisis — if you refuse to repent, then it becomes deadly,

24

but if you repent, it becomes an opportunity to a great spiritual breakthrough.

I have been there from time to time before. This is not condemnation from the enemy, but genuine convictions from the Lord. Sometime it's both. The solution to this spiritual crisis isn't positive thinking or distraction, which leads to false peace but real spiritual danger, but to really humble ourselves like David and ask for help and forgiveness:

"Wash me thoroughly from mine iniquity, and cleanse me from my sin. For I acknowledge my transgressions: and my sin is ever before me. Against thee, thee only, have I sinned, and done this evil in thy sight: that thou mightiest be justified when thou speakest, and be clear when thou judgest. Behold, I was shapen in iniquity; and in sin did my mother conceive me." Psalm 51:2-5

In the scripture above, David is specifically confessing his adultery and homicide before God. He goes very deep this time, even trace back to when he was still a fetus. Then, he goes on to ask for restoration of the joy of salvation! It clearly indicates that David knows that salvation is not automatic, nor is it "once saved always saved":

"Restore unto me the joy of thy salvation; and uphold me with thy free spirit. Then will I teach transgressors thy ways; and sinners shall be converted unto thee. Deliver me from blood guiltiness, O God, thou God of my salvation: and my tongue shall sing aloud of thy righteousness."
Psalm 51:12-14

On the other hand, David knows that God will forgive and deliver him from his sins if he sincerely asks for it. He didn't just believe and confess some easy, general, and broad term sins in a one-size-fit-all, one-and-only-once-in-a-lifetime prayer, but he actively seeks forgiveness from God when God convicts him of specific transgressions. Do I Still Need to Repent After I become a Christian?

The following passage will make it clear.

"Have I any pleasure at all that the wicked should die? Saith the Lord GOD: and not that he

should return from his ways, and live? But when the righteous turneth away from his righteousness, and committeth iniquity, and doeth according to all the abominations that the wicked man doeth, shall he live? All his righteousness that he hath done shall not be mentioned: in his trespass that he hath trespassed, and in his sin that he hath sinned, in them shall he die. Yet ye say the way of the LORD is not equal. Hear now, O house of Israel; is not my way equal? Are not your ways unequal? When a righteous man turneth away from his righteousness, and committeth iniquity, and dieth in them; for his iniquity that he hath done shall he die. Again, when the wicked man turneth away from his wickedness that he hath committed, and doeth that which is lawful and right, he shall save his soul alive. Because he considereth, and turneth away from all his transgressions that he hath committed, he shall surely live, he shall not die".
Ezekiel 18:23-28.

If the wicked turn away from his transgressions, he shall live. But if the righteous turn away from God's grace and forgiveness, but sin deliberately and die in them, then he dies in sin!

27

In summary, if one has been living in sins for 10 years, then even though he was saved before, he would have ended up in hell if he died during those 10 years. If the period of unrepentant last only 10 minutes, it's still a window of vulnerability when the sinner might die in sin during that 10 minutes and thus go to Hell.

Does it sound scary? Isn't it too scary to be possible? Read this verse below.

"Remember therefore how thou hast received and heard, and hold fast, and repent. If therefore thou shalt not watch, I will come on thee as a thief, and thou shalt not know what hour I will come upon thee." Revelation 3:3

This verse talks about how we should watch out for the Rapture. But the principle is the same for salvation. We don't know when we will die, so it is wise to stay out of willful and prolonged sins lest we die in them.

How Do I Know That I Am Saved?

You can be sure of your salvation **today**. As long as you are not refusing to repent of any known sin, as long as you have a good relationship with God, and as long as you believe that salvation can only be obtained by grace, through faith, in our Lord and Savior Jesus Christ, then you can be absolutely certain that you are being saved. If by accident you die at this moment, you are going to heaven.

How Do I Make Sure That I Am Not Going To Die In Sin?

We can all learn from David's prayer, *"Keep back thy servant also from presumptuous sins; let them not have dominion over me: then shall I be upright, and I shall be innocent from the great transgression."* (Psalms 19:13).

This is a matter of faith. If we always worry about the future, what we worry about will tend to come true, but if we have faith in God, His power will manifest. Have faith in God and His words. Study God's word and proclaim His promises frequently. The more you do it, the more truth will sanctify you, change you, and strengthen you. (John 17:17; James 1:21; 1 John 1:7)

Your willpower and best intention in the present can never guarantee the final condition of your heart, not even the present condition! Only the power of biblical faith, which can unleash the power of God, can accomplish that. That's why we have to pray, praise, fellowship with other Christian, and study the Bible diligently. The more we do them, the more likely that we can endure to the end because these activities can increase our faith, cover our blind spots, keep us close to God, unleash the power of truth, and help us retain more truth.

And finally, *"May God himself, the God of peace, sanctify you through and through. May your whole spirit, soul and body be kept blameless at the coming of our Lord Jesus Christ?"* (1 Thessalonians 5:23).

Jesus saith unto him, **I am the way............,** Our Lord takes the opportunity of this discourse

about the place he was going to, and the way unto it, more fully to instruct his disciples concerning himself, saying, **"I am the way"**; Christ is not
merely the way, as he goes before his people as
an example; or merely as a prophet, pointing out
unto them by his doctrine the way of
salvation; but he is the way of salvation itself by
his obedience and sacrifice; nor is there any other;
he is the way of his Father's appointing, and
which is entirely agreeable to the perfections of
God, and suitable to the case and condition of
sinners; he is the way to all the blessings of the
covenant of grace; and he is the right way into a
Gospel church state here; no one comes rightly
into a church of Christ but by faith in him; and he
is the way to heaven: he is entered into it himself
by his own blood, and has opened the way to it
through himself for his people: he adds, the truth
he is not only true, but truth itself: this may
regard his person and character; he is the true
God, and eternal life; truly and really man; as a
prophet he taught the way of God in truth; as a
priest, he is a faithful, as well as a merciful one,
true and faithful to him that appointed him; and
as a King, just and true are all his ways and

administrations: he is the sum and substance of all the truths of the Gospel; they are all full of him, and Centre in him; and he is the truth of all the types and shadows, promises and prophecies of the Old Testament; they have all their accomplishment in him; and he is the true way, in opposition to all false ones of man's devising. And this phrase seems to be opposed to a notion of the Jews, that the law was the true way of life, and who confined truth to the law. They have a saying (r), that, "Moses and his law are the truth"; this they make **Korah** and his company stay in hell. That the law of Moses was truth, is certain; but it is too strong an expression to say of Moses himself, that he was truth; but well agrees with Christ, by whom grace and truth came in opposition to Moses, by whom came the law: but when they say (s),, "there is no truth but the law", they do not speak truth. More truly do they speak, when, in answer to that question, "what is truth?" it is said, that he is the living God, and King of the world (t), characters that well agree with Christ. And the life: Christ is the author and giver of life, natural, spiritual, and eternal; or he is the way of life, or "the living way"; in opposition to

32

the law, which was so far from being the way of life, that it was the ministration of condemnation and death: he always, and ever will be the way; all in this way live, none ever die; and it is a way that leads to eternal life: and to conclude all the epithets in one sentence, Christ is the true way to eternal life It is added by way of explanation of him, as the way, no man cometh unto the Father but by me; Christ is the only way to have access unto the Father; there is no coming to God as an absolute God, not upon the foot of the covenant of works, nor without a Mediator; and the only Mediator between God and man is Christ: he introduces and presents the persons and services of his people to his Father, and gives them acceptance with him. God help us….. Amen.

Chapter Two

DO THE WORK OF AN EVANGELIST

"But watch thou in all things, endure afflictions, do the work of an evangelist, make full proof of thy ministry" 2 Timothy 4:5

1.   **Keep prayer for those aren't yet followers of Jesus central to church life**

What we pray for tends to reflect what we value, hold as important. Ensuring that in our prayers we continually pray about our sharing of the faith and pray for those who don't know Christ will help keep evangelism central. How about training all those who lead intercessions on a Sunday to do this well. Or having this as a prayer point always in your church prayer group, home

34

group or children's group to pray for this every time you meet?

2.   Lead by example

In my little work as an evangelist it was sadly rare the number of times those in general church leadership brought people to campus evangelistic campaigns I was speaking at. Part of our role is to lead by example, to **'do the work of an evangelist'** (2 Timothy 4) even if we aren't evangelists. I know it isn't easy, but that is the point. If we are having a go at playing our part in God's ongoing work of evangelism in his world we will much more easily understand the struggles others are having as well. And what people see us do they will see as important.

3.   Tell honest stories

It is great to hear stories from those who have come to faith, and we need to tell these as often as possible to encourage people God is still at work drawing to himself. But it also helps to tell honest stories of when things didn't go as we hoped: the person we invited to God who said they would come and didn't turn up; the spouse who we've been praying for over many years who seems no closer. These stories told will help people to know it isn't easy, but we must persevere none-the-less. Why? Because at some point in our own lives God wrote people into our stories who he used to help us come to faith, and he longs to do the same through us.

4. Teach people how to show and share their faith

Most Christians feel lost for words. Most are fearful of not knowing what to say. I think we can help people play their part in God's work of evangelism by ensuring they know the answers to three questions:

What is my role in evangelism?

How do I fulfill that role?

How do I keep motivated?

How each church answers these will vary, but our role as leaders of our various churches is to ensure there is a clear answer for each and that we equip people in the light of these answers. Then everyone can play their roles assigned or given. There are a range of resources around to help equip people to share their faith, and even a simple approach can bear fruit. One preacher I know laid on two evenings a month apart where he covered some basic ideas on faith sharing, and I was so encouraged by the stories that were told at the second evening about ways God had been at work already. Let us put in our efforts brethren in Christ and win the lost at all cost, let us invest much in evangelism and by so doing we will achieve results in fishing for men...

The Evangelism Gift
The evangelism gift holds a very unique place among the spiritual gifts. In many ways, it is the most "unstable" of all the gifts. When it is **"on"** it is the pastor's best friend. Who doesn't want to see more non-Christians coming around our churches? But when it is **"off"** it can be a thorn in the side of the pastor. How many frustrated evangelists are challenged to lead in our local churches? The gift is calling out for attention, investment, and the opportunity to win lost people to Jesus.

Pastors who guide the mission must remember that the evangelism gift can be a bit "moody" (pun intended). If the gift is not utilized, it can be dormant, scowl a bit, and make life challenging for all on the team. But when it is used and allowed to operate, the team is much stronger for it. We must make an extra effort to develop the evangelism gift in local churches. **J. Robert Clinton** at Fuller Theological Seminary teaches the evangelism gift is the first spiritual gift to lose its power. It is often the first gift to atrophy. As we guide the mission, may our mantra concerning the evangelism gift be, **"Use it or lose it!"** Below are some thoughts on how to make the evangelism gift work for you, your leadership, and the growth of your church. *"J. Robert Clinton, Unlocking Your Giftedness (Altadena: Barnabas Publishers, 1993), p. 269"*

Closers and Harvest Events
In the world of sports, there is a term that applies to players who are able to help their teams win close games. These are the players who hit the game-winning jump shot, make the crucial pass, or strike out the opposing batter with runners on

base. These players who excel at the end of games under incredible pressure are known as **"closers"**. The closers seem to have a different personality than the rest of the players on their team. Closers want the ball when the game is on the line. They absolutely relish the big moment where the difference is victory or defeat. The same is not true for everyone on the team.

In many ways, the evangelists in your church are like closers from the sports world. They have a different spiritual outlook. They have a DNA that is often different from a person gifted to be a pastor or Bible teacher. These people are drawn to, and even yearn, for the moment of helping people move closer to committing their lives to Jesus. These people have been wired and spiritually gifted by God, to explain the gospel and help non-Christians commit to Jesus. They are amazingly valuable assets to your church ministry team. Sadly, many evangelists are neither identified nor developed in the local church. Many are faithful, serving, loving leaders in our churches, but they are not doing what they are gifted by God to do.

As a pastor who guides the mission, I would commend that your church create events and services where every Christian who has been telling the story of God can bring their non-Christian friends. At these events, your **"closers"** can tell the story of Jesus, share their own stories of conversion, and skillfully call for commitment. By hosting evangelistic events, you not only help develop your evangelists, you will likely reach more non-Christians and create a positive culture of regular evangelism in your local church. (Please see the article *"Evangelism and the Church Calendar"* for further thoughts and details).

Developing Public Evangelists
As pastors who guide the mission, here are practical leadership steps that you can take to help identify and develop those with the public gift of evangelism.

Calling All Evangelists
I find it interesting that most local churches invest significant time and resources in training pastors and helping to develop their preaching

associates. Young preachers are carefully selected, given quality resources to write sermons, and provided with ongoing support and mentoring. Leaders are readily available when crisis hits. We do leadership development very well for leaders who lead their fellow Christians.

But how do we carefully select, resource, and provide ongoing support for the evangelist? One could even argue that the evangelist has a much harder ministry task than the preacher. The evangelist is preaching to someone who is not familiar with church, likely has many questions, and is under the power of Satan.

We would do well to intentionally seek out and identify who have the evangelism gift in our churches. It would go a long way to gather those people, empower them with a vision for using their gifts, and to help them mature as evangelists. Sadly, evangelists in many churches are never called, gathered, nor invested in.

Biblical Evangelism Models

The growing evangelist needs models and a game plan for growth. The evangelist must be an overall student of the Bible. But they should especially study the passages related to Dr. and the process of salvation. They should have deep in their ministry quiver the arrows of how Jesus called for commitment. They should be ready to quickly recall phrases and sermon content of the first evangelists in Acts. And they should be able to process this eternal truth and contextualize it into your local setting.

Historical Mentors

The history of evangelistic preaching is rich and abounding. We must help our young evangelists commit their current ministry to the great tradition of the church. Our developing evangelists must become familiar with the greatest preachers and winners of souls. Sitting under the evangelism ministries of Charles Spurgeon, Billy Graham, David Brainerd, Watchman Nee, and the countless heralds of God, will expand their gift passion and help them see what is possible.

Calling for Commitment

The young evangelistic preacher must take special interest in learning how to call for commitment. It is a common mistake for young evangelists to speak the majority of their time in the pulpit and rush the commitment. A wise evangelist will give ample time at the conclusion of their sermon and communicate in such a way that helps people process the myriad of emotions that come with commitment. The preacher must be aware of the work of the Holy Spirit and learn to partner with God in calling home lost sheep.

How this looks in your context is one of the great riddles of evangelistic preaching that is waiting to be solved. But once it is figured out, and done well, the preacher not only calls home sinners, but he is now modeling for all the congregation how to help people commit to Jesus. May you help the young evangelists not only experience evangelistic preaching, but more importantly, to learn from their own experiences.

I bless you with the same blessing that Paul gave to Priscilla and Aquila. They came across an

amazing orator and evangelist named Apollos. But he needed seasoned leadership, mentoring, and theological training. Luke tells us that Priscilla and Aquila took him and explained to him the way of God more accurately. (Acts 18.27)
May God use you to encourage and raise up an Apollos in your own congregation.... Amen

---

Chapter Three

SPEAK WITH AUTHORITY AND COURAGE

Matthew 11:11-12 *"Assuredly, I said onto you, among those born of women there has risen one greater than John the Baptist; but he who is least in the kingdom of heaven is greater than he. And from the days of John the Baptist until now the kingdom of heaven suffers violence and the violence takes it by force"* (NKJV)

Today multitudes of unbelievers are hurtling along a wide avenue to hell, they chant, they dance, they wine and feast. They do not give a hoot about the gospel we preach! Many of us Christians today sit unconcern, where we are fully sentient of the realities of sinners going to hell. I on one occasion visited the **morgue** at the **Tamale Teaching Hospital** were the Lord extraordinarily anointed me and commission me as an evangelist unto the nations of this world. Something very weird and wonderful happened to me that I will want to speak about in this book, as minutes and hours went by, lifeless bodies are been carried to the morgue. I stood by and watched as natives, brought in departed relative, these people were distressing and stunned, you must know that only a few hours or minutes earlier they had been talking to a living human, who was now departed forever. I noticed that there did not appear to be any particular time of the day when dead people are not brought to the morgue and, for the first time am seeing this scenes I was very terrified and shaken there Jesus whispered to me and said *" son these are people I died for, I shed my blood for them I gave up everything for their sake, but how many of them do you believe are saved?, in they valor, passion and zeal I commission you today as an evangelist unto the nations of this earth, go declare my good news and salvation to them all reminding them*

46

that I am coming in a little while...". You see my brethren in Christ, humans have a short time to live on this earth and what so ever we do with our lives today determines where we will go after death, brothers and sisters Hell is real, please let us escape it by living righteous lives and also preaching the good news of Christ to the untold that they might also be saved, we have a short time to live after which our mortal remains will go back to the dust but our souls continue to live on and will be judge according to our deeds and works when we were alive on earth, we are strangers on this earth and we must live as such. This reminds me of a documentary I have watched on human anatomy and in that documentary you will see how human beings are been dissected like animals and some their internal organs are been taken out to prevent the dead body from decomposing, others are also used as practical for medical students at the universities in fact it is a sad experience and I never want to watch that documentary again it looks so horrible. This shows how we humans need to live righteous lives in Christ Jesus, there I have come to the conclusion that a lot of people die across the city

47

and nations of the world all the time, death happens at indiscriminate. A person who has never visited the morgue will not know how common death is, how frequently people depart into eternity!

Today many of our church service fellowships, revivals, get-togethers and fastidious songs are not sufficient to win the masses to Christ, what are you doing as a minister, a believer, a shepherd to save souls from entering hell fire, are you tranquil or serious?. You have to rise up and go into the world and make disciples of all nations and educate them what Christ has taught you, do not be stimulated by the circumstances around you. As I said earlier on, souls are hurtling along the road of destruction. They do not even know that they are going to hell. This is the lot of unbelievers today, they listen to the music of the devil, the melodies and lullabies of this present world, charm them. Because of these things, they do not know that they are walking in their own destruction; they do not even care whether Jesus comes today or tomorrow, they will say *"leave me alone, to hell with these church matters of yours"*. This is why you need to apply vigor. Many people are blinded by the devil; we must unlock their eyes to the realities of heaven and hell. 2 Corinthians 4:4 says *"... the god of this world hath blinded the minds of them..."* Apostle Paul did not only preach nice sermons, he aggressively involved in revolving the heads and opening the eyes of unbelievers. I always recognize when people are ignoring the word of God, but dear readers I do not want anyone to ignore this word of God am sharing with you in this book, I must turn people to the right path and open their eyes to the truth. On one particular occasion my friends and I were approached by a Muslim friend on campus complaining to us about a brothers wife who was suffering from an infirmity which have been treated for a while but have since not left and he continued by saying *" I have seen the great works God is using you to do on campus here and I think and believe that if you go to pray for her, she will be healed"* The I immediately asked him if he believes in then sovereignty of our Lord and master Jesus and he said yes; then the holy spirit ministered to me in the words *"I need you to turn their hearts to me*

49

and I will heal them of their diseases". I obeyed that instruction; so we told him to call his brother and inform him of our coming, so that evening we left school to the brother's house and my dear readers, when we got there the ladies condition was very terrible but we believed in our hearts that our God was a God of possibilities. Then I asked the man and the wife if they are willing to accept Jesus Christ as their Lord and personal savior that was after I preached the good quality news of John 3:16 to them and I also told them that Jesus was the only and only one who can heal her wife from that disease. Then the man and his wife and brother who took us to the brother's house all lifted their hands and accepted to be saved after which we lead them to pray the sinners prayer after which I asked the woman if she believes that Jesus can heal her which she said yes she believes. So we prayed and glory to the name of the Lord who called us to work at his vineyard the woman received healing and we were so thankful to Jesus.

So as a preacher, an evangelist you do not wait for the people to come to church you will end up preaching to yourself, go to the people because the gospel of Jesus Christ is go ye therefore but not wait for them to come. My dear friends in Christ and all readers, let us stop playing the buffoonery, if we are going to preach the gospel let us not preach to ourselves, lets, go out there and drive and force them to the Lord's house. Hallelujah

Chapter Four

KEEP BROADCASTING THE WORD OF GOD

"Go ye therefore and teach, all nations, baptizing them in the name of the Father, and of the Son and of the Holy spirit; teaching them to observe all things, whatsoever I have commanded you, and lo, am with you always, even unto the end of the world". Mathew 28:19-20.

"But ye shall receive power, after the Holy Spirit is come upon you; and ye shall be witnesses unto me both in Jerusalem, and in all Judea, and in Samaria and unto the uttermost part of the earth" Acts 1:8

When Jesus said go and make disciples of all nations, He did not specify a group of people but he was referring to you and I. today many souls are moving down the broad road to hell as stated in the previous chapter, but they do not know, they are being blinded with the things of this world, that is why Jesus instructed you and I to preach the gospel to all creation. What are you doing as a man of God, as an evangelist, and the church as a whole?, Today you see churches spending a lot of money to build schools, hospitals and so on. I am not saying that those things are not good but the truth is that they are not the primary duties of the church but rather secondary duties, so the primary ones needs to be achieved first and the secondary follows. Today we see pastors driving in expensive cars, living in big mansions and eating their choice of delicacies. Today, churches and their leaders have run away from their primary duties and doing all kinds of things that do not help in the propagation of the gospel to all, not even the truth is been preached to the congregation, pastors today preach more of blessings and prosperity messages than preaching on how one can obtain salvation and how one can enter into heaven and escape hell fire, today you see pastors asking for money and other gifts from members before they pray for the, even some pastors have allowed themselves to be used by the enemy, they have conform to the desires of the flesh and going to the extent of even sleeping with some of the young ladies in their church. The primary role of the church is spiritual and soul winning but not to build schools and hospitals, the church and its associates must invest much in evangelism and soul winning crusades. Things that do not conform to what Christ has instructed must be stopped now.

The Bible says you shall receive power, when the Holy Ghost has come upon you and you shall be witnesses of Christ to all creation, the question is, are you doing the witnessing? The answer is a big no, today if you tell some pastors to go to a village like *"Tengilento"* in the northern part of Ghana to pastor a newly established church, I bet you he will refuse and tell you that the conditions there are not favorable enough to live in, that community, he will bring before a lot of excuses and reasons why he would not go to that part of this country but he has forgotten that his calling into the ministry is to propagate the gospel to those who have not heard of Jesus and not to stay In the cities and enjoy but rather have a sense that there are many souls who have not heard about the gospel of Jesus Christ and are perishing. I tell you the truth today if you are a man of God and you are not working for the reason to which you have been called, you will surely see hell fire.

How many of us speak to at least one unbeliever about Christ in a day? , how many? It is a pity that we are not doing our primary duties as Christians.

A sister once told me that, her pastor will always preach about prosperity in every church service, and will always request for financial support from church members and even at times borrow from them, can you imagine that. And because of this reason she has stop going to church and she will never go to any church again because she thinks all the churches are the same. A pastor who is supposed to expand and fill the church, now through his own selfish interest the church members are now leaving the church. A pastor is supposing to preach the gospel but not to be requesting and borrowing monies from his congregation.

My friend in Christ the time has come and it is now, we must rise up to the task as believers to win the masses who are lost to Christ, Bible says **"he that wins souls is wise"** amen.

The promise of the Holy Spirit has been received as believers and so therefore if we do not preach the gospel to unbelievers and win them for Christ, if we do not tell them the truth and they die in their ignorance, brethren I tell you the truth their blood will be require from you. (Ezekiel 3:18). Brethren rise up with the tenacity of a mountain goat and proclaim the good news of Christ, the time is now or never, pastors and leaders of the church you have to stop preaching more on prosperity and preach salvation, preach the truth, preach about a certain heaven and a certain hell to your congregation before they are taken unaware. Before they will say **"had I know"**. The prophet of God Hosea says **"for lack of knowledge my people are destroyed"**. If you are a pastor and you allow your members perish, I tell you the candid truth you will also perish. (Jeremiah 23) do not miss lead the church and the children of God, win more souls out there for Christ and you will be reward in this generation and the new world to come Amen. Arise today and seek the expansion of Gods kingdom for he has anointed you with the power of the Holy Ghost and also given you power and dominion over the enemy to do his work so therefore nothing can stop you, move now with the power and the anointing of the Holy Ghost. Jesus said in Luke 10:19 **"I have given you power, authority and dominion to trend upon serpents and scorpions and all powers of darkness and nothing by any means will harm you"**.

Do not waste the power of God in your life, utilize that power today. Win the lost at all cost today, the world needs you now! God helps us... Amen.

Chapter Five

THE ANOINTING OF GOD IS UPON YOU

"The spirit of the Lord God is upon me; because the Lord hath anointed me preach good tidings unto meek; he hath sent me to bind up the broken hearted, to proclaim liberty to the captives and opening of the prison to them that are bound; to proclaim the acceptance year of the Lord and the day of vengeance of our God; to comfort all that mourn" Isaiah 61:1-2.

The spirit of the Lord is on every believer once you are born again, men of God, you have been anointed by God to preach the good news to all flesh, but today many anointed ministers have deviated from the actual call of God, because

58

they have given into the desires of this age. The love for money is now gaining roots in their lives and they will say *"soul winning should wait, God has not called me to preach repentance, but prosperity, he has not called me to preach salvation, so I don't need to go win souls"*, you can see that the desire of the flesh has over powered the task God have given to such people, you need to allow the spirit of God to reveal to you the mind of God and the mind of God is to populate his kingdom. And so you have to first choose the things of the kingdom of God. Do not be a worker of God because of your own selfish gains and ambitions but rather work for God according to your calling and purpose. Do not let anybody (enemy) deceive you, because he knows he has a limited time to rule and he wants a lot of people to his side. But you have to save yourself and others from entering hell fire because you have been mandated to set at liberty the captives free.

As a Christian you cannot be deceived because the truth is reviled in your heart. You can only be deceived for as long as you stay outside the real teachings and calling of God. Many are lost and they need to hear and know about the man called

Jesus, for the bible says; *"faith comes by hearing and by hearing the word of God"*. God have anointed you to preach the good news, the world needs you now. Just as fire burns the body, that is the same way fornication and adultery does to the body of some believers and unbelievers without their knowledge (1 Corinthians 6:18).I tell you the truth committing adultery is like taking fire into your cloth and fornication is like walking barefooted on burning coal but people are ignorant about these realities, you have to tell them, you have to liberate them for they have been kept captive, the unbelievers and some believers who are still struggling with sin needs your help, go and preach salvation unto them.

As I have witnessed to people over the years, I have come to know that nothing exposes a man to satanic slavery than sinful sexual communion. You see that these people are enslave to sin, they need your help, they are in the bondage of the enemy, they are wallowing in sin, they are seeing hell fire and so they need somebody, pastors, you need to rise up to the task and win a lot for Jesus. Statistics have shown that about **90%** of our

60

youth today are into fornication (premarital sex); and this has become a reality even in our regional capital here in Tamale where a young man slept with close to fifty ladies took pictures and videos of them and posted them on the internet and this is not the only incident in our country you go to our secondary schools, tertiary institutions and it will interest you to know that sex has become a norm among the youth not only Ghana but the world at large. I still remember a lady telling me that at a certain point in your youthfulness you need to have sex or else you will become outmoded, can you imagine that! The youth of our world today are lost and need to be brought back to the right path because fornication brings a provocation of heavenly sentence for your abolition. Can I tell you the candid truth in a manner that you may not want to hear it? Young ladies hear me, if you are found of opening up yourself for any man to have sex with you, hell will open its mouth and swallow you up, so flee fornication. *"Every sin that a man, doeth is without the body, but he that committeth fornication sinneth, against his own body"* (1 Corinthians 6:18)

Many of the youth are expose to things of this wicked generation, their minds have been polluted and the only thing they need now is the word of God and you and I have been assigned to do the propagation of the gospel and so you have to avail yourself for God to use you today, to save his people from hell fire. Friends in Christ, today many unbelievers ignorantly sell their future for just a minute of sex, even some Christians are involved in this, and most people call this act pleasure not knowing very well that it will bring them pressure in the end. Carnality is a magnet to catastrophe, sex outside marriage is accessible for them on the streets for just a cedi or dollar. But they do not know the truth. The truth is that, this is just an insignificant recompense that gets naive people to contemplate that it is cheap. The real cost of sex before or outside marriage is hell. It may come in two parcels; explicitly hell before death and hell after death, some believers do not even know this truth, and they always at times commit this kind of sin. And now that the truth have been reviled to you in this book, please go ahead to still have sex with individuals you are not married to. My dear brethren convey adequate discipline with you and every devil will give way at the sight of you. God have sent you, he has empower you, he has given you the strength to set at liberty the captives free and the time is now, even thou it will be difficult but with determination, perseverance and hope in God you will overcome for his anointing is upon you, God will stand by you, that you will not fall into temptation, do not be moved by circumstances around you, the environment in which you find yourself in and the people around you, should not be an obstacle to you but let your focus and hope be on God. Friends in Christ you need to know where you are in Gods time table for your life, where are you? Are you in Gods purpose now? The answer is yes because the Bible says; God has anointed you to preach his word.

A few years ago **Rev. Park Yong Gyu** of south Korea had a revelation to hell and heaven, and he said; *"the masses are in hell than in heaven, so many souls are perishing in hell, and the angel of the Lord said to me that the ratio of heaven to hell in a day is a thousand to one"* this simply means that thousand people enter hell and just a single human being enter heaven in a day, this is a very sad story and this ratio must be changed now!, hell must not dominate the kingdom of heaven, this revelation must ginger us to win the lost at all cost and seek the expansion of Gods kingdom, before things get out of hands, use the anointing that has been given to you, the hour is hear and it is now, rise up now and receive the infusion of the courage of a lion and win souls for Christ. Amen

Chapter Six

EVERY BELIEVER HAS A ROLE TO PLAY IN EVANGELISM

"... All must share alike: whoever stays behind with the supplies gets the same share as the one who goes into battle." 1 Samuel 30:24. (GNB)

The above scripture is to all Christians and followers of Christ Jesus, you need to support your pastors, your church or youth group or adult groups, Sunday schools, evangelism campaigns etc. through prayers, which is very important, you have to pray for your pastor as he is trying his best to win souls, you must support in prayer, financially and if there are other resources you can offer to help in evangelism.

You need to pray and intercede for your ministers and evangelist of God who are doing everything possible to win the masses to the house of
God. You have to know that, these soul they are
trying hard to win are been trapped under the
bondage of Satan and the only way they can be
won is to fight and contend with the devil for
those souls, and by so doing you and I need to
pray fervently for soul winners and it is our responsibility to do so, because we wrestle not
against flesh and blood, but against principalities,
rulers of darkness and spiritual wickedness at
high places and with this reason the Apostle Paul
a man of prayer in his generation, asked for prayers from his congregation;

Romans 13:30, *"Now I beseech you brethren for
the Lord Jesus Christ's sake, and for the love of
the spirit, that ye strive together with me in your
prayers to God for me"* and the verse 31 says *"that
I may be delivered from them that do not believe
in Judea; and that my service which I have for
Jerusalem may be accepted of the saints"* .

You see that! This was the request made by the great apostle of God, this implies that the men of God around us needs our prayers and this is the role that God has given to you, so therefore my dear readers, you have to pray now! This is the duty assigned to you in the soul winning business, yours is not to mount the pulpit, because everybody cannot mount the pulpit at a time, so therefore you need to be operating behind the scenes. If you have ever watched behind the scenes of a movie, you have, noticed that the activities of the movie crew contribute a whole lot to the success of the movie. As a viewer, you may not have seen the camera men, make-up artists, sound personnel and costumers; but the truth is, without them, the movie would not have been in existence. Today you must know that without your help, without your contributions, your pastor's quest for soul winning will not be effective, your contributions are needed in your church, and your prayers and intersession for your pastors and evangelist are so, so important for them in the quest of soul winning, maybe you did not take part in the open crusade and other soul winning programs but through your prayers they will become successful. So my friends in Christ even if you are not in the lime light, even if you are not recognize, even if you are not popular still remain faithful in playing your role assigned to you, though your bishop is the head of the church but still help him because he cannot do everything, you will have to pin hands with him, keep doing what God asks you do and never give up, keep doing, help your leaders in their soul winning campaign and God will continually reward your faithfulness. Apostle Paul in many of his writings writes about waging war against the Kingdom of Satan, he said in Ephesians 6:12 that *"we wrestle not against flesh and blood..."* Paul was indeed a man of prayer but he also depended greatly on the prayers of his congregation. Prayers are very important in the life of a soul winner, the Apostle Paul made yet another request that, his congregation should pray for that his ministry would be accepted. So therefore my brethren in the Lord, we must and we need to pray fervently for our ministers that through their ministrations, many souls will be won. 2 Corinthians 4:3-4 *"... the god of this world hath blinded the minds of them..."* you see that! The minds and thoughts of the unbelivers have been blinded by Satan and they don't not eve relies it, their hearts have been hardened and they don't even know it and they are not aware that they walking in their own destruction in view of the above scripture, the work of an evangelist has become very difficult, so therefore you and I have a role to play and thus by praying fervently for our men of God in the ministry of evangelism and through our prayers, God will revel unto them, what they should say. Men and Women of God are not supposed to be preaching *"Cork and Bull"* stories but to preach the word of God with have power and also the word that God have revel unto them and also to preach the mysteries of God and what God has commanded them to do. When we read the book of 1Thessalonians 1:5, *"for our gospel come not unto you in word only, but also in power and in the Holy Ghost and in much assurance; as ye know what manner of men we were among you for your sake"*.

Over here what the apostle of God was saying is that, we must preach the gospel and the word of

God that is so powerful and convincing enough to bring to the house of God the lost souls and also the words out of our mouths should bring hope and conviction unto the people we minister too. Rise up to day and seek the expansion of God's kingdom now! Hallelujah.

You need to work hand in hand with your church leaders to achieve a common goal and whatever work you are doing in the house of the Lord it will never be forgotten, in the realms of the spirit it will stay forever, God will use you to do a permanent work by the power of the anointing. You have a role to play in the soul winning business.

2Corinthians 9:7 *"every man according as he purposeth in his heart, so let him give; not grudgingly, or of necessity; for God loveth a cheerful giver"*.

God is unwilling to abandon a cheerful a cheerful giver. In other words, God always locates such a person and intervenes in any situation that concerns him or her, you see that if you support in God's work, if you support in evangelism wholeheartedly God will bless you, his love will be upon you. Givers are very special to God and this is why you must continually give. Be cheerful always when you give something to help in the kingdom business and do not grumble, because cheerful givers always move the heart of God.

you see, the Bible records in Luke 7, that the Jewish elders pleaded with Jesus to heal the sick servant of a roman centurion and we know that the ordinarily, the Jews should not have anything to do with this centurion, because he was not a Jew, but because he was a cheerful giver, they pleaded on his behalf (Luke 7:4-5). And Jesus followed them immediately when he heard all they did, if you will help in the house of God, if you serve your leaders. One day even your enemy will wish you well, your enemy will endorse you when a good opportunity is available.

Service is most likely your dominant style if the following statements best describe you:
(1)   I see needs in people's lives that others often overlook.

71

(2) I find fulfillment in helping others, often in behind-the-scenes ways.

(3) I would rather show love through actions than through words.

(4) I have found that my quiet demonstrations of love and care sometimes help people open up and become more receptive to what I think.

(5) I think the world would be a better place if people would talk less and take more action on behalf of their friends and neighbors.

(6) I tend to be more practical and action-oriented than philosophical and idea-oriented.

If you have responded, "That's *me!*" to these six statements, then you are representative of the *Serving Style*.

Such people have a tendency to be others-centered, patient, willing to work behind the scenes, and typically demonstrate love through their actions, rather than through mere words alone. Again, it is hard to find many *negatives* with respect to people who simply want to *love one another*, and who seek to do so in a quiet, unassuming manner.

The biblical example is that of **Tabitha (Dorcas)** in Acts 9:36-42. This woman lived in Joppa, and **"was always doing good and helping the poor."** One of her talents was making clothing for the poor, a gift for which she was well-beloved in that area. Following her death there was much grieving among the widows, to whom she had apparently been a great blessing. The apostle Peter was summoned and he raised her from the dead. *"This became known all over Joppa, and many people believed in the Lord."* Not only the miracle of her restoration to life, but the grace of her service while living, had touched many people's lives. Tabitha was truly the embodiment of the *Serving Style* of evangelism, and she was most effective in her ministry. Not all evangelism has to be showy or dramatic. Sometimes just simple acts of loving charity will do more to reach the lost than just about anything else. After all, as the saying goes, *"people don't care how much you know, until they know how much you care!"* Tabitha cared -- so she served -- and she won souls to Christ Jesus. Rise up today, receive the spirit of service through that you can win the lost for the kingdom of God...God help us.

Chapter Seven

BE SERIOUS WITH EVANGELISM

"And he said unto them, go ye into all the world, and preach the gospel to every creature" Mark 16:15.

Soul winners are very treasurable and famous people in the sight of God. As a child of God, a servant of God nothing should mean more to you than leading those in your planet who have not yet known our Lord and master Jesus into salvation. This is something you must take very seriously this particular time, more than ever.

2 Corinthians 5:19 says; *"to wit, that God was in Christ, reconciling the world unto himself, not*

imputing their trespass unto them; and hath committed unto us the world of reconciliation".

You see that! God has committed to you the ministry of reconciliation; not only did he call you into the fellowship with his son Jesus *(1corin. 1:9);* he is also calling us to partner him in soul winning. Jesus needs you to win a lot of souls, be serious with this great commission, and get serious with it now! Romans 12:11 *"we are admonished not to be slothful in loneliness, but be serious in spirit, serving the Lord".* Am talking about being serious in Gods number one business and that is soul winning. You will always experience ever more blessings, success and progress in this present time and in the new world to come as you engage in soul winning activities. Humans are Gods greatest assets on earth, until you start winning people for Jesus; you are not involved in Gods asset building project.

Through you God will always reach out to the unsaved, to touch their lives with his power and glory; so avail yourself now so that this can be done through you; therefore pastors and church leaders you must always be passionate about soul winning.

To be active and effective as a soul winner, you must be able to see beyond your present circumstances; you must see beyond every limitation and refuse anything obstructing your views in this great responsibility of ours today. Arise and get rid of all destructing influences and fervently serve the Lord as a soul winner for all your life. It is your purpose for being a soul winner. Apostle Paul said in his letter to the Corinthian Church;

1Corin. 9:16 that; *"for though I preach the gospel, I have nothing to glorify of; for necessity is laid upon me, yea, woe is unto me, if I preach not the gospel!"*

My brethren in Christ keep saying the word of God where ever you are, it is the right thing to do, never allow yourself to be deceived, because God wants you to preach his word, but know that you will face persecutions but you will still win, amen! *"Yea and all that will live godly in*

Christ Jesus shall suffer persecution" 2Timothy 3:12.you sees that! , persecution is a promise for every believer in Christ, it is necessary for your promotion and it will come to you in different levels in your Christian life. It is what makes you different from others and separate you from the masses; persecution is the harsh treatment from others to compel you to comply with their own ways of doing things. As a good Christian who lives by Gods word will surely be persecuted no matter what be the case, Jesus confirms this in

John 15:20: *"remember the words that I said unto you, the servant is not greater than his LORD. If they have persecuted me, they will also persecute you; if they have kept my sayings they will keep yours also".*

Any human person who wants to preach the gospel must be ready to face persecutions as Jesus did. But brethren the most beautiful and interesting thing is that, as you remain standing and being faithful to Gods words, irrespective of what you are going through, the good Lord himself will honor you. Jesus knew that we will encounter challenges and problems in this world as we preach the word of God, but he also said that as we remain in him, we would live a life of peace even in the day of adversity.

"These things I have spoken unto you, that in me ye shall have peace. In the world ye shall have tribulations; but be of good cheer, I have overcome the world" John 16:33.

you may wonder why Jesus left us in this world of trials and temptations or wants to know why he allows trials to come our way in this life, the truth is that God does not mind about trails and temptations coming your way since he knows he has already made you more than a conquer. (Romans 8:37). Rise up and conquer your enemies by winning more souls.

1 John 4:4 says; *"Ye are of God little children, and have overcome them, because greater is he that in you, than he that is in the world"*

You have to expect persecutions and never be afraid of it, believe in it, it is important. The more you face persecution, the measure of persecution that you face is the measure of training you have, irrespective of all kinds of tests, persecutions, trails and temptations that you might face in your quest for soul winning and the work of God, rejoice; for they will be bread for you, all such contrary winds will only drive your roots deeper in God, go all out and win the lost souls without fear or panic.

You have to take charge of everything, the bible says whosoever is born of God overcomes the world; and this is the victory that overcomes the world, even our faith! I want you to know something, when you study about the life of Jesus and the way and manner he responded to different problems and circumstances; you will realize that he is always in charge. His language was that of faith and absolute mastery. He is always in control of affairs and unperturbed by anything, his words were powerful and he displayed an attitude of rest in the midst of turmoil and my brethren this is the life Jesus has given to us believers to live after. You must learn to be unruffled or unperplexed, regardless of what is happening around you. Take charge now, preach without fear, and act like Jesus, who remained on moved when he was told in the book of John 11:3; **"... Lord behold he whom thou lovest is sick"**. You will notice that he was not moved by the news of Lazarus' sickness, he remained unflustered even when he was told that Lazarus had died and had been buried for four days, you could see that Jesus was in charge, you have to also take charge of certain things now!.

When Jesus eventually showed up, Mary and Martha at different occasions came to Jesus and said; **"Lord if you had been here, Lazarus our brother would not have died"** am often thrilled at Jesus' response, with neither regret nor hassle in his speech, he said;

"I am the resurrection, and the life: he that believeth in me, thou he were dead, yet shall he live: and whosoever liveth and believeth in me shall never die... ". John 11:25.

What confidence; when others were extremely confused and agitated! How I love that man

Jesus, nothing could shake him! Hassle-free he stood at the entrance of the sepulcher, voiced a simple prayer of thanks to the father, and called out in a loud voice; **"Lazarus come forth"** and the Bible says the man that had been dead for four days came out alive. John 11:41-44. he was in total control, you have to imitate Jesus, pastors and leaders this is the wakeup call for you to rise up and get serious for the expansion of Gods kingdom, take control, relaxed, the power is in your hands, go on never stop and do not be moved at all. Jesus practiced faith at the highest level, functioning at a place of rest and absolute mastery. Faith recognizes no fear because it trusts in the ability of God. When you are faced with challenges in soul winning do not cower. Be in charge. All the days of your life, irrespective of what happens around you, even if you receive negative news from afar, maintain you composure and declare Gods word, take charge now refuse to worry; just give the world an effective change Now!... God help us..

Chapter Eight

STAND TO YOUR GROUNDS IN EVANGELISM

"Watch ye, stand fast in the faith, quit you like men, be strong".1Corithians16:13.

Soul winners must be strong and firm in faith at all times. Some people are in effective in their Christian walk because they are burdened by the care and desires of this life, and this act choke Gods word in their hearts and dissipate their faith (Mark 4:18-19).One of the many things you must be resolute about this present day is to stand firm in faith, by setting your heart on God; give him your undivided attention and do the evangelism to the highest level of which you can.

Proverbs23:26 says; *"my son, give me thine heart, and let thine eyes observe my ways"*. *And in Proverbs4:20 also says; "my son, attend to my words; incline thine ear onto my sayings"*. Why is this important? , Why does the Lord require you to give him your heart and incline your ear onto his sayings? It is simple, because faith comes by hearing and by hearing the word of God (Romans 10:17).For your faith to grow and prevail you have to attend to God's word and incline your ears unto his sayings, you have to focus and give attention to the word in your life. The necessary results of this are that your thoughts, words and actions will be in connection with the word, making you unshakable. Go all out and proclaim the good news about Jesus. Many vacillate are unstable in their lives because they give room to too many destructions instead of attending to his word, never allow anything to sway your confidence away from God. Jesus said in Luke 21:34 *"and take heed to yourselves, least at any time your hearts be over changed with surfeiting and drunkenness and cares of life, and so that day come upon you unawares"*

Pastors and all believers, it is your responsibility to take charge of your hearts and stop yourselves from veering off course. Be on track for God, be aglow for Christ, go into the harvest field now and start harvesting, harvest more souls as you can, do not limit yourself, be motivated always by the number of souls you win. The coming of our Lord is near and it is important to win the masses and keep our eyes on the goal, standing firm in faith. This is not the time to vacillate or cower but times to focus on doing the masters will and fulfill his call on your life. *"Therefore my beloved brethren, be ye steadfast, unmovable, always abounding in the work of the Lord, for as much as ye know that your lab our is not in vain in the Lord"* 1 Corinthians 15:58,

Put on the whole amour of GOD at all time, because soul winning is a battle. Ephesians 6:11: *"put on the whole amour of GOD, That ye may be able to stand against the wiles of the devil..."* in our fight of faith, soul winning and propagation of the gospel. The bible says;

"...we wrestle not against flesh and blood, but against principalities against powers, against the rulers of darkness of this world, against spiritual wickedness in high places" Ephesians 6:12,

That is why we are enjoined to put on the whole amour of God, there is no use praying and crying to God to protect you as an evangelist or his servant, God have told you what to do, put on the amour of God. You have been mandated to put on the amour of God but not some of it; you are not to leave any part of that amour;

*"Wherefore take unto you the whole amour of God that ye may be able to withstand in the evil days..."*Ephesians 6:13-17,

You are to have your loins covered with truth, wear the breastplate of righteousness, have your feet shod with the gospel of peace, wear the helmet of salvation, and put on above all the others, the shield of faith. That is the shield with which you extinguish all fiery darts the devil throws at you. The amour of God is available to you this day, go for it now as you prepare to go into the battle with the enemy as to who is going to populate his kingdom *(heaven or hell)* you have to make conscious efforts and choices to put the amour of God on, go for it and be a soldier of Christ and win more souls. Keep it on at all time. The hand of God is upon you, no weapon formed against you shall prosper and every tongue that will accuse you shall be condemned. Do the street evangelism without fear. **2Corin. 3:6;** *"who also hath made us able ministers of the new testament, not of the letter, but of the spirit; for the letter killeth, but the spirit giveth life"*.

You will remember in the Old Testament the prophet Joel foretold what will happen in the lives of Gods people when they receive the Holy Spirit.. *"...Your sons and daughters shall prophesy ..."Joel2:28*.

Notice he did not say *"...they shall keep shut up..."* but *"they shall speak words of power"*. Evidence that you have received the Holy Spirit is when the gospel of Christ is your number one passion; when you preach it with boldness, because it is fire, shut up in your bones.

"But ye shall receive power, after the Holy Spirit is come upon you and ye shall be witnesses unto me both in Jerusalem, and in all Judea, and in Samaria and unto the uttermost part of the earth" **Acts 1:8.**

Part of the ministry of the Holy Spirit in your life is to strengthen you to function as an able minister of the gospel. After apostle peter received the Holy Spirit his fears disappeared. The once "unlearned fisherman" began to say and do supernatural things, so much so, that in one day , through his preaching, three thousands souls were converted. Perhaps, you have experienced so much pressures and persecutions from preaching the gospel, and now you feel like giving up; do not be discourage, do not keep quiet. When Jeremiah preached the word of God he was severely persecuted by those around him, and was eventually put into prison, he examined.

"... but his word was in mine heart as a burning fire, shut up in my bones, and I was weary, with forbearing and I could not stay" Jeremiah 20:9
There should not be enough discouragement in

this world, to stop you from preaching the gospel. Anywhere you will find yourself, open your mouth and let them know that salvation has come; that God is not mad at them, and that they can now embrace life and immortality through the gospel. Get serious now.

May God bless you as you are ready to seek the expansion of His kingdom, and turn to the voice of God now! Hallelujah. Be very, very, committed to soul winning and you will be blessed forever Amen.....

Chapter Nine

WHEN ARE SOULS WON?

"There is a difference between soul winning and discipleship. Soul winning happens in an instant, discipleship takes a lifetime."

This seems to be the biggest misunderstanding of the whole subject. The Christian church today are completely blinded to knowing exactly when or how a soul is won. The reason again, is because most people have not studied the subject of soul winning. They just have a strong belief of what it is and without true knowledge of the subject, tend to speak their mind. Have you ever heard of the old saying, **"I never talk about politics or**

religion"? People make this statement because they have never studied the subject of politics, taken time to study the ins and outs of each political party, and its beliefs. They have shaped their views about specific political parties because someone they are closed to and trusted encouraged them to believe a certain political party. The same thing is true about religion. Most people in the world today, believe it or not, have not studied the word of God.

Yes, some have read it; some have studied portions, but in general, most have not actually studied the whole word of God. People do, how-ever, have very strong beliefs on what is right for salvation and making it to heaven. People believe certain ways because someone from their family, or close friend, or someone in their life that they trusted told them something and they accepted it without truly searching the scriptures to know the truth for themselves, Acts 17: 11 *"these were more noble than those in Thessalonica, in that they received the word with all readiness of mind, and searched the scriptures daily, whether those things were so".*

We must approach the subject of soul winning in the same careful manner. We must study to show ourselves approved. We must know for certain what the word of God says!

The Bible gives us a clear picture of when a soul is won. In the book of John, Jesus outlines the formula to being born again:

John 3:5 Jesus answered, *"Verily, verily, I say unto thee, except a man be born of water and of the Spirit, he cannot enter into the kingdom of God".*

When someone is born again, they become a new creature in Christ. They are purchased with a price, the blood of the lamb! At the point someone is born again, that soul has been won to God. A lot of people ask me the question, *"Well, what if someone is born again one night and the next night they backslide? Are you saying that their soul has still been won?"*
The answer is yes. Once a soul has been born, it

cannot become un-born. When someone backslides, it does not negate the birth. There is a difference between soul winning and discipleship. Soul winning happens in an instance, discipleship takes a lifetime.

When someone is born again of the water and the spirit, they are born again. Everything that happens after the new birth is discipleship and walking with the Lord. We are not saved until we hear those wonderful words of our savior, "Well done."

Some people are won to the Lord and sadly after many years of living for God, they backslide. That doesn't mean that their soul was not won, it simply means they didn't endure until the end. In order to win the lost and grow our churches, we must understand that we must reach the lost, we must win souls, and then we must disciple them. I have heard the saying many times, **"Well bless God, what good is it to pray all those people through and baptize them if they are not going to stay?"** Usually this is something of an excuse, meaning were not going to go win the lost because people don't stay. The answer is not to neglect the harvest. The answer is we must win souls and disciple them! I always ask the people who use that excuse some questions. I say, *"By the way, out of all those who were baptized and prayed through, how many of them did you personally go visit? How many of them did you personally invite to your home for dinner? How many of them did you personally teach a Bible study too? How many did you personally call and make sure they had a ride to church?"*

The answer is always the same: *NONE!* We have to understand something about soul winning. When someone is born again, they become as a baby in the eyes of God. Spiritually they become newborn baby! The statistics tell us, that if we brought a newborn baby home from the hospital and laid the child in a bed without touching, feeding, or caring for it in any way for three days, the child would not survive it would die. The same principle applies to spiritual babies. We cannot pray people through, baptize them in Jesus' name and send them on their way with a letter from the pastor thanking them for coming.

We cannot expect them to survive!

We must get involved in their lives. We must personally make sure they are cared for, that they are notified of church services, that they have a ride, that they are visited and invited to our homes. There is an old saying that says, *"People don't care how much you know until they know how much you care!"* We must love our new babies and protect them! So basically it takes three things to win a soul:

1. We have to find someone who is lost and compel him or her to repent and be baptized in Jesus' name.

2. The person has to be willing to surrender to God. They have to be willing to make a new start and repent of their sins and be baptized in Jesus' name.

3. It takes a God with mercy to forgive them and fill them with the Holy Ghost. This is when the increase is given. Once those three things are finished, we have personally won

a soul.

Some people have made the statement, **"Well, some plant and some water."**

They say this suggesting that they just play a part in soul winning, and they do not personally ever win a soul this could not be further from the truth. It is a deception from the enemy to keep the people of God from winning the lost!

There are certainly times that we will plant seed, and other times when we will only water. But, we are instructed to go, compel, and persuade the lost. We must personally win souls.

For instance, let's say I am out on a soul-winning mission. I am looking for sinners to talk to and I come across a young man sitting on a bench. If I hand him an invitation to our church and he says he will try and make it sometime, did I win a soul? Of course not, I just planted a seed, he was not born again. Another time I may see someone out at the market. I begin talking to him or her and invite him or her to church. As I am speaking, they begin to cry and feel conviction, so I compel that person to come immediately to the church to repent and be baptized in Jesus' name. The person agrees to come. We take them to the church, we repent, we then baptize them and we ask God to fill them with the Holy Ghost. At this time, they did not receive the Holy Ghost. Did I win a soul? No, it takes being born again of the water and the spirit to be born again. God chose not to give the increase this time, so basically I only watered.

But sometimes we must win someone! There are many times when the person comes and repents, they are baptized, and God fills them with the Holy Ghost to give the increase!

Some people are deceived to believe that just because they are in a certain ministry in the church they are playing their part in soul winning. Therefore they are not required to go out and win the lost. This is another form of deception. For instance, a lady who plays the music for the church claims she is a soul winner because she is the minister of music. Sorry, that is not soul winning. That is music ministry. Someone says, *"Well bless God; I am the Usher in the church. I do my part to win the lost by making sure there is order in the house of God."* That is awesome, but that is not soul winning. That is ushering. Someone might say, *"Well bless God; I am a soul winner because I go out on outreach and hand out invitations. Well that's a great thing to do, but that is not soul winning. That is planting seed."* Someone says, "Well, I am a soul winner because I teach Bible studies to all the new converts. "Well, thank God for that ministry of teaching but that is not soul winning. That is teaching. Someone said, *"Well I am a soul winner because I am the pastor and I pastor all of these people."* Well that is awesome and we need pastors, but the Bible tells us the five-fold ministry is for the perfecting of the *saints* not soul winning! We absolutely need every one of the ministries listed above in our churches. They are very important; however, we cannot say they are soul winning when in reality they are given for discipleship. Again, soul winning only happens when you personally go out and find someone who is lost and compel him or her to repent and be baptized and God gives the increase by filling him or her with the Holy Ghost! If we can get this understanding, can you imagine how many more souls will be back in the fields of harvest seeking the lost? I do not want one soul to be lost. I pray that each person reading this book will get a true understanding of soul winning and allow God to use you to reach multitudes of souls! Everywhere you go there are lost souls. All you have to do is take time with them, love them, listen to them, and compel them to repent and be baptized. In return, God is going to fill them with the Holy Ghost and give the increase. We also must understand this to help solve a huge problem we face today with Holy Ghost Crusades. I am all for seeing every soul receives the gift of the Holy Ghost, but if that person speaks in tongues for ten hours and gets hit by a car without being baptized in Jesus' name, they have not been born again of the water and the spirit. We must compel people to *both* be baptized and filled with the Holy Spirit! Don't be afraid to compel them to be baptized. You may be surprised at how many will get in the tank right then! The Bible says there is no promise of tomorrow. We must do what we can to persuade people to be saved. Rise up to day and seek the expansion of God's kingdom now!

Chapter Ten

WHO OUGHT TO WIN A SOUL?

"There is no church or ministry that exempts us from winning the lost."

This is always a very serious subject. First let me say, I cannot visualize some people trying to wiggle their way out of winning others. Soul winners keep people from an eternal life of torment.

In Acts 1:8; the Bible proclaims we will receive a power to become witnesses. It does not give exclusions to anyone. As a matter of fact, God is no respecter of persons. What one must do, we all must do. One of the things that we will have to learn as leaders is that people will only follow

100

you where you are willing to personally go. If you are not willing to win souls yourself, how do you expect people following you to win souls? There is no ministry that exempts us from winning the lost. As a matter of fact our whole ministry should revolve around reaching the lost and the efforts to disciple people. When we received the Holy Ghost, God gave us a power to become witnesses. He instructed us to go and reach the lost. Once we receive a calling to a particular ministry, we cannot lay aside our main mission to reach the lost to focus on our ministry. We must have a balance, and on one side of the scale it should be soul winning and personal evangelism alone. On the other side of the scale should be everything else in your walk with God such as prayer, fasting, studying, ministry, etc....

A lot of people say to me, *"You're out of balance with all your talk about soul winning."* *I often ask them, "If I'm out of balance with soul winning, when was the last time, you personally won a soul? You're out of balance with ministry."* We must maintain a balance of both.

Some people use the saying, "Well sheep begot sheep and because I'm a shepherd, I don't have to win souls, just the Saints need to!" To be honest, this type of statement, in my mind, is almost blasphemous! How can we think we are exempted from reaching the lost because we have become shepherds? Jesus was the greatest shepherd of all yet, he gave his whole life to winning souls! Also every pastor or shepherd I know also has a pastor in their life, which makes them a sheep as well! Every person is called to ministry. When a person comes out of the water, they should be placed in some type of ministry. This will keep them active and on fire for God. One of the greatest ministries to get someone involved in as a new convert is soul winning. People who just come to the Lord have a fresh fire and want to tell everyone what they know about their experience. There is also no age limit exempting us from soul winning.

I hear a lot of times that a person is too young or too old to win souls. This is another deception of the enemy. If the enemy can keep us from winning the lost, he that many more souls to

Hell. If you are old enough to receive the Holy Ghost, you are old enough to receive the power to become a witness! Someone said, *"Well bless God, what about the 85 -year-old elderly sister that can't get out in the streets to win souls, but she spends hours in prayer for people. Are you saying she is not a soul winner?"* Sadly *yes*, she is not winning souls by praying. She is doing an awesome job in that calling; however, there is no exemption for people to avoid winning souls. We need the elderly to pray for souls, but they also must be active in winning souls. As a matter of fact, sometimes the elderly can be more effective at winning the lost than anyone else. For instance, do you remember going to your grandma's house as a child? Maybe you were there with your mother and when you did something wrong your mother threatened to beat you or correct you. Just in time, grandma stepped in and said, *"You're not beating that baby at my house!"* There is something about a grandma or grandpa figure in our life that expresses mercy. No matter how mean a person is, usually when they are approached by an elderly figure, they tend to calm down. I understand this is not 100 percent of the time, but for the most part it is accurate. So when a grandma approaches a sinner and asks them to repent, usually that person will be more than willing to listen and obey. Also, a lot of older people were brought up in the era of the church when outreach and soul winning were more common. A lot of these elderly people, believe it or not, want to get back in the fields of harvest! Children are the same. If we are ever going to reach this world, we are going to have to train up this next generation of children to win souls. We cannot afford to place our children in segregated classrooms and keep them from sinners, teaching them to shun people who are lost. We must get our kids out of the play land and into the streets to win the lost. You would be surprised to know how effective a child can be at witnessing and winning the lost. It's very hard for someone who would normally reject an adult to reject a sweet little child! I have watched for many years; mothers of church children guard them and protect them from people just because they are sinners! We must teach our children to love the lost and reach for every soul! Another huge mistake, in my opinion, is putting our children in private schools and keeping them from children who are lost. How are we ever going to shine our light into the dark world if everyone around us is supposedly saved? In most cases when I find someone who has never won a soul since being born again, they tell me the reason is because they are scared, they are shy, or they just fear the rejection of someone telling them no. The last excuse is probably the number one excuse I hear. People who are making that excuse truly don't know what they're saying. You see, the Bible tells us that God has not given us a spirit of fear! The enemy of our soul gives you that spirit so you operate in bondage, preventing you from reaching the lost. The enemy gives people the spirit of fear. It is no different than an addiction to drugs and it is a bondage that shackles people to sin. You might say, *"Well, I'm not sure it's sin."* *The Bible says,* *"He that knows to do good and does it not."* Is a sin! You see, when the enemy gives you that spirit, you are held hostage to the spirit of fear, never doing God's will, reaching the lost. The enemy actually wins. You have to be delivered from that spirit the same way

105

someone who is held captive to drugs or alcohol is delivered! God is ready to deliver you today. Be honest with him and he will set you free! Again, how can someone with the Holy Ghost want to avoid winning others from the eternal damnation of hell? For every person you reach, that's one more person that doesn't have to spend eternity in a lake of fire with eternal torment! Pray and ask God to give you a fresh passion for souls! Ask him to lead you to the lost in your city! The fields are white! Will you respond?

Chapter Eleven

PLACES TO WIN SOULS

"Some claim they do not want to be in the violent neighborhoods because they do not feel safe. How will these lost souls ever see the light if the people with the light take it and hide it?"

Everywhere you go, you should be looking for an opportunity to win someone to God. The fields are white. There are so many souls ready to come, that there are not enough soul winners to get them all! The key to winning and being sensitive to souls is praying. Ask God before you leave your home or church. *"Lord, lead me right to the hungry person you want to save today."*

Almost every time I pray that prayer, God leads me to someone that is hungry and hurting and needing God! When you are out, you can even tell the person you approach,

"Listen, before I left my home I prayed and asked God to send me right to the person he wanted to save today, and guess where God sent me to out of all the people in this city? That's right, that's how much God loves you, and he sent me right to you!"

Everywhere we go is a mission field; there are people in every direction that need God.

Restaurants are a great place to win souls. I cannot tell you how many of our Christian servers at this place have won, just by being nice to them and leaving them a generous tip! Schools are another place for young people to win their friends and classmates. Believe it or not, young people are truly looking for God! Don't let this opportunity pass you by! Church events and services are a great place to win souls. Find the new guests and go to them and compel them. The people who come to church are looking for more than a night of entertainment. Money exchangers in Ghana popularly known as *"black market"* is another great place to reach people because usually the people doing the transaction have plenty of time to listen to what you say! One of the things we have learned in reaching the lost is that just as in the days of Jesus, the hungry are the poor, blind, captive, broken-hearted, and hurting people. It could be possible that we are not winning the lost because we are selecting whom we want to win instead of who is ready to be won. Sometimes we hear people boasting of how they invited their lawyer or doctor to church, putting a star trophy on the wall. That doctor or lawyer may never attend, while we ignore the ten poor people already on the pews who are starving for a touch of God.

If we neglect the poor and hurting people of our cities, we are neglecting the biggest part of the harvest. People rarely come to God when everything is going good in their life. We have upgraded our churches in the bad neighborhoods to multi-million dollar facilities to entertain the church people while leaving the lost to a life of sin without hope. Some of our churches are so nice, sinners feel uncomfortable and the lost have no transportation to get there. We almost make it impossible sometimes to reach the lost by our desires to fit in with the mainstream churches. Some claim they do not want to be in the rough neighborhoods because they do not feel safe. How will these lost souls ever see the light if the people with the light take it and hide it? If you move your church to a multi-million dollar facility, at least start a daughter work in the poor areas of town so those souls have somewhere to attend and be ministered too. Most people do not attend church because they have no way to get there. Why not start church plants in every area of the city so people can walk to church! I always have said that there would not be bad neighbor hoods if the enemy of our souls had not tricked us into the spirit of fear, believing we were in danger. Had the church not been afraid, we could have been bringing the people of the bad neighborhoods to Sunday school over the last 10 years and they would have grown up with a passion for God! This is probably the hardest chapter for me to write, I just want to stay everywhere and end it! I don't think I can think of one place where you cannot or should not try and win souls! Never give up in soul winning rise up and win the lost at all cost.

Chapter Twelve

ENCOURAGEMENT TO SOUL WINNERS

"We must fight the spirit, not the people! Love everyone, even those who talk about you! Pray for those who speak against you... love them even more!" Galatians 6:9

"And let us not be weary in well doing: for in due season we shall reap, if we faint not."

I have wondered at times why anyone would become weary in well doing. As I became more passionate about souls and reaching the lost, I have learned to understand more about this scripture. One would think, as life tells us, that good things happen to those who do good. We

112

should consider, though, we are working in the spiritual realm. We are fighting devils and pulling people from hell! We are fighting an enemy that is terrible in every way. He is out to steal, kill and destroy us! I have talked to other soul winners and heard many stories of some terrible things that happen in the lives of soul winners. We must be careful not to become weary in well doing! We shall come against fierce opposition. The enemy of our souls will use unexpected people to talk about you, plot against you, and even try and cause you physical harm! I don't want to cause anyone to become frightened, but listen; soul winning is not the easiest job on this earth! We must always remember that our reward will be in heaven! Sure, we will rejoice with sinners as they pray through, but we shall also fight battles for their souls! People will feel convicted. Many people are not doing what they need for God, so when they see you reaching souls they have to get you down to their level. Many will gossip, lie, and cause you many unpleasant periods. We must keep a good spirit and not react in a negative way. The devil is waiting for you to get angry and say something

113

nasty to someone so he can try and beat you down with guilt and shame and slow your work down. Don't be ignorant to the devils devices! The Bible does not leave us powerless over these attacks.

Ephesians 6:12 **"For we wrestle not against flesh and blood, but against principalities, against powers, against the rulers of the darkness of this world, against spiritual wickedness in high places."**

We must fight the spirit, not the people! Love everyone, even those who talk about you! Pray for those who speak against you...love them even more! Keep a good attitude, do not argue and get angry over anything people will do. One way to that will help you is to keep your weapons sharp! Pray and fast often, read the word of God, praise God and worship him during the trials. I know it will be hard to do, but this is the way the scriptures teach us to do battle! The weapons of our warfare aren't carnal! This means we do not attack our brothers and sisters! We must pray even more for them! One other thing that is so important to a soul winner's **success** is to stay in touch with other soul winners. We are in this together, and many have fought similar battles! We need each other! Learn to gain strength from your fellow soldiers! When we are down, we need to be lifted up through the love and compassion of our brothers and sisters. Take time to encourage people who are soul winners. Go out of your way to bless them. You never know what they may be going through! We can make a difference in our world! We can bring souls out of the lake of fire! The price is not cheap, but the blessings aren't worthless! Reach your community. Go with passion. Love your neighbor as yourself! The Bible is clear, we must reach the lost. If you are working to reach souls, you are in the will of God! Keep working, keep reaching, the last part of the scripture is our promise, **"for in due season we shall reap, if we faint not."** Rise up with the tenacity of a mountain goat and win the lost at all cost … Amen.

Chapter Thirteen

ENDURING TO THE DAY OF JESUS' SECOND COMING

'Who can endure the day of His coming? Who will stand when He appears?' (Malachi 3:2). 'When the Son of Man comes, will He find faith on the earth?' (Luke 18:8). 'See that you do not refuse Him who speaks. If the ancient people did not escape when they refused Noah who warned on the Earth, how much more will we not escape who turn away from Him who warns us from heaven' (Hebrews 12:25).

The Bible speaks a lot about the dreadful suffering and ordeal the whole earth will be forced to endure before Jesus comes again. **'In those days**

116

there will be great oppression, such as there has *never been from the beginning of creation until* *now and never will be again'* (Mark 13:19). The emphasis is on enduring, which is not always an enjoyable situation. Persecution is never enjoyable but if we are to follow Jesus, we will suffer persecution and we need to be prepared to endure right to the end. Jesus warned us, *"Remember the word (warning) I said to you, 'A* *servant is not greater than his Lord. If they* *persecuted me they will also persecute* *you'"* (John 15:20). Jesus said several times, only those who endure to the end will be saved. Those who turn their backs on God before the end may go to a lost eternity. *'You will be hated by all* *people for my name's sake, but those who endure* *to the end will be saved ... Those who endure to* *the end will be saved'* (Matthew 10:22; 24:13). *'You must endure hardship as a good soldier of* *Jesus ... If we endure, we will also reign with* *Him. If we deny Him, He will deny us'* (2 Timothy 2:3 & 12). *'Only through many afflictions can* *we enter the Kingdom of God'* (Acts 14:22). The people who believe they will be 'raptured away' before great tribulation comes are most at risk because when terrible times come, they will not be prepared, so start preparing yourselves for that day because there is no going to be rapture before the great tribulations. Only those whose hearts are prepared will be able to endure the tribulations right up until the Great Day of Jesus' return.

Persecution is only one difficulty we will face before Jesus comes back. We will also suffer financial losses, family breakdown, sickness that may never be healed, changes in weather patterns, lawless behavior, violence, robberies, freakish accidents and many other trials before Jesus returns. It is not because God wants people to suffer but suffering comes as a result of the lawlessness, violence and the ungodliness of the majority of the world's population, which is increasing at an amazing rate. **'When the wicked increase, sin increases'** (Proverbs 29:16). God never intentionally causes suffering or affliction. **'He does not willingly afflict or grieve the children of men'** (Lamentations 3:33). It is the vast array of sin throughout the world that causes misery, affliction, sickness, strife, wars and persecution. It does not come from God. A lot of suffering comes from sin, the consequences of our own sin or the consequences of sin against the innocent committed by evil men. One of the reasons the Lord sent Noah's flood to destroy all of mankind was because of violence.

'The earth was corrupt before God and the earth was filled with violence' (Genesis 6:11). If there is violence committed by evil men, then there are those who suffer as the innocent victims of violence. Jesus warned us lawlessness or iniquity would increase and the love of many Christians would wax cold before He returns. **'Iniquity will be multiplied and the love of many will grow cold'** (Matthew 24:12). The Lord hates violence of any kind, especially against women and children, and violence against women and child abuse are on the increase. *'I the Lord love justice. I hate robbery with violence' (Isaiah 61:8). 'I hate divorce and marital separation, and a man who covers his wife with violence. Therefore keep a watch upon your spirit so you do not deal treacherously and faithlessly with your*

wife' (Malachi 2:16). **'Cursed is the man who harasses, vexes or denies justice to the foreigner, the fatherless and a widow'** (Deuteronomy 27:19).

There is another reason why Christians in particular will suffer terribly the closer the time comes for the return of Jesus. **'Woe to the earth and to the sea because the devil has gone down to you in great wrath, knowing he has only a short time ... Permission was given to the devil to make war with the Christians and to overcome them. Authority over every tribe, people, language and nation was given to him ... If anyone has an ear, let them hear ... Here calls for the endurance and the faith of the Christians'** (Revelation 12:12; 13:7,9 & 10). Those few verses are very frightening but it is written in the Bible and Christians must be able to heed the warning and keep their faith no matter what circumstances may arise. Those Christians, who have a spiritual ear, let them listen to the warnings in the Bible, be very watchful and careful.

In these last days, all believers need to be genuine

disciples. Jesus said go and make disciples of all people. He never said to make church members. There is no scripture in the Bible telling us to sign a form to make us church members or fill this form to become a church member. We are accepted members of the collective Body of Jesus because we are washed in His blood, baptized in water and in the Holy Spirit. **'Go and make disciples of all nations, baptizing them in my name, teaching them to observe all the things I commanded you'** (Matthew 28:19 & 20). Any church that does not accept people because they have not signed a piece of paper are not walking according to the scriptures and may be discarding true disciples. Church attendees who are not disciples are counterproductive. They give the world a very incorrect view of the whole salvation message and a totally false impression of what our Messiah Jesus and the cross is all about. The full Gospel contains information regarding the cross with the shedding of Jesus' blood, the second coming, holiness, denying ourselves, the Kingdom of God and other truths Jesus taught, and anything that leaves out these aspects of discipleship is a falsification of the Gospel of Jesus.

The erroneous modern teaching saying we will have nothing but happiness, prosperity, joy, health and wealth is not the foundation of the Gospel message. Many Christians are healthy and wealthy, but that is not the foundation of the Kingdom of Heaven. The foundation message does not major on human self-centeredness but it majors on Jesus as the Son of God, our Messiah, our Savior, His miraculous birth, the ministry and teachings of Jesus, the blood of Jesus, the cross of Jesus, His suffering, His sacrifice for us and His resurrection preceding the resurrection of the righteous on the last day as we enter the Kingdom of Heaven. Yes, the Kingdom of God was open to us when Jesus first began His ministry (Matthew 12:28; John 3:3), but it is only after we are found worthy on Judgment Day will we enter the Kingdom of Heaven (John 3:5). Seeing the Kingdom of God and entering the Kingdom of Heaven are two different situations. Seeing the Kingdom of God is like looking through a window to see what is inside.

Entering the Kingdom of Heaven is going into the room through an open door that will be shut to sinners and to those who were not ready. *'While they were away (complacent), the Bridegroom came and those who were ready went in with Him to the marriage feast and the door was shut'* (Matthew 25:10).

We relate to Jesus' suffering by our suffering, knowing it helps us develop endurance and perseverance. *'We rejoice in our sufferings, knowing that suffering works perseverance. Perseverance produces character. Character produces hope and hope does not disappoint us because God's love has been poured out into our hearts through the Holy Spirit who was given to us'* (Romans 5:3 to 5). If we suffer with Him, we will be glorified with Him (Romans 8:17). *'It is commendable if someone endures pain, suffering unjustly because of their conscience toward God ... When you do well and you patiently endure suffering, this is commendable with God. To this we were called because Jesus suffered for us, leaving us an example, we should follow in His steps ... Jesus suffered for us in the flesh so arm yourselves with the same mind ... Beloved, do not be astonished at the fiery trial which has come upon you to test you as though a strange thing has happened to you, but because you are partakers of Jesus' sufferings, rejoice ... If you are insulted for the name of Jesus, you are blessed ... If one of you suffers for being a Christian do not be ashamed'* (1 *Peter* 2:19 to 21; 4:1, 12 to 16). That is what it means to be a genuine disciple of Jesus. Suffering is part of our walk with God and we need to be prepared to endure increasing suffering, trials, afflictions and persecutions the closer we are to Jesus' second coming. It is good to keep in mind, all the trials we endure help purify us and make us fit for the Kingdom of Heaven and for that we need to thank God (Colossians 1:12).

God has not lowered His standards of holiness, mankind has lowered theirs. This is how God describes people in the world who have rejected Him. He gives them up. *'God gave them up to the lusts of their hearts, to uncleanness so their bodies would be dishonored among themselves. People who exchanged the truth of God for a lie and worshipped and served the creature rather than the Creator who is blessed forever Amen.*

For this reason, God gave them up to vile passions. Their women changed the natural function to what is against nature. Likewise the men, leaving the natural function of the woman, burned in their lust toward one another, men doing what is inappropriate with other men and receiving in themselves the due penalty of their sin. They refused to acknowledge God, so He gave them up to a depraved mind to do those things which are loathsome, being filled with all unrighteousness, iniquity, greed, sexual immorality, malice, wickedness, covetousness, jealousy, murder, strife, deceit, cruelty, slanderers, backbiters, hating God, insolent, arrogant, proud, boastful, inventors of all things evil, disobedient to parents, without understanding, faithless covenant breakers, heartless, without natural affection, unforgiving, unmerciful, who knowing the decree of God for those who practice such things are worthy of (eternal) death, not only do the same but approve of those who practice them' (Romans 1:24 to 32). How should we react to people who behave so badly? We need to have the strength to rebuke their behavior and share the Gospel with them. We love the person but hate their sin. Jesus died for them just as sincerely

125

as He died for the righteous, but we are not to fellowship with them. *'Have no fellowship with the unfruitful works of darkness but rather reprove them. The things done by them in secret is a shame even to speak of but all things, when they are reproved, are revealed by the Light, for the Light reveals everything'* (Ephesians 5:11 to 13). *'What fellowships have righteousness and iniquity? What fellowship has Light with darkness?'* (2 Corinthians 6:14).

'My people are destroyed for lack of knowledge' (Hosea 4:6). Many Christians are unaware of what God wants from them and if they continue on their present path, they may end up spiritually destroyed. What is God trying to achieve with mankind? He wants His own special people to love and have fellowship with and God will do whatever it takes to achieve His goal and that includes shaking the earth to its foundations (Isaiah 24:19). To be accepted into the Kingdom of Heaven, every believer must be ready at His second coming. Jesus' first coming was to prepare people for eternity by bringing the Kingdom of God to earth and His second coming will

be to rule the earth for one thousand years then the righteous will inherit the newly created earth. All those who accept Jesus are being formed into a special group of people He is purifying for Himself, for His own possession (Titus 2:14). The Jewish people were the first nation called to be God's own special people. *'If you will indeed obey my voice and keep my covenant, then you will be my own possession from among all peoples. All the earth is mine. You will be to me a kingdom of priests and a holy nation'* (Exodus 19:5 & 6). Through the blood and cross of our Jewish Messiah, that invitation to be God's chosen to join with the Jewish people has been extended to Gentiles who once had no hope and no mercy. *'You are a chosen race, a royal priesthood, a holy nation, a people for God's own possession so you may proclaim the excellence of Him who called you out of darkness into His marvelous light, who in times past were no people, but now are God's people, who had not received mercy but now have received mercy'* (1 Peter 2:9 & 10). *'You (Gentiles) were separate from Jesus, alienated from the commonwealth of Israel and estranged from the covenants of the promise, having no hope and without God in the world, but now in Jesus, you who once were far off are made near in the blood of Jesus'* (Ephesians 2:12 & 13). Gentiles will never replace the Jewish people in God's affection, but we have been invited to join with the Jewish people to be God's elite alongside them.

God gave Jesus to us to redeem us from sin and to purify for Himself His own special people (Titus 2:14).

'Everyone who has the hope of salvation in them purifies themselves just as Jesus is pure' (1 John 3:3).

Notice the emphasis is on purity. Titus said God purifies us; John says we must purify ourselves. It is a two way process. God works in us and together we achieve His goal. Jesus purifies us with our cooperation. He will not purify us if we refuse to cooperate. The Lord is coming for a spotlessly pure, holy Bride (Ephesians 5:27) and we must be ready. *'Let us rejoice and be exceedingly glad and give the glory to Jesus, for the marriage of the Lamb has come and His Bride has made*

128

herself ready' (Revelation 19:7). Many unsaved people are beginning to mock the theory of the Second Coming because they feel Jesus has not appeared, therefore He never will. The Scriptures said people would become rebellious over this fact. *'Know this, in the last days mockers will come walking after their own lusts saying, "Where is the promise of His coming? ...* **All things continue as they were from the beginning of the creation'"** (2 Peter 3:3 & 4). Their rebellion does not alter the fact we must be ready. Our responsibility is to do what God has already commanded us and that is to purify ourselves and be ready for His return.

When Jesus was on earth, He did not know when He was going to return but warned us to watch, be vigilant, be prepared and we must not be complacent. *'Of that day or that hour no one knows, not the angels in heaven nor the Son, but only the Father. Watch, keep alert and pray, for you do not know when the time will come ... Watch therefore for you do not know when the Lord of the house is coming, whether at evening, or at midnight, or when at dawn, or in the morning, lest coming suddenly He might find you sleeping (complacent). What I tell you, I tell all. Watch'"* (Mark 13:32 to 37). If Jesus did not know the time and date of His own return, then we should be content not to know until it is time for us to know. We are not going to miss out if we obey and prepare ourselves. If anybody declares they know when Jesus is returning, they are deluding themselves and misleading others. They are a false prophet and Jesus said several times, we must not believe such things and must not go there. *'There will arise false messiahs and false prophets, and they will show great signs and wonders so as to lead astray, if possible, even the elect (Christians). Behold, I have warned you beforehand. If they tell you, 'He is in the wilderness,' do not go out, or 'He is in the inner rooms,' do not believe it. As the lightning flashes from the east and is seen to the west, so will be the coming of the Son of Man'* (Matthew 24:24 to 27). We must remember, Jesus taught when He comes, everyone will know about it because every person on earth will see Him (Revelation 1:7). Jesus is God and He is therefore omnipresent – literally everywhere at once, so every eye will see

Him all at once. That is how we will know He has arrived and there will be no mistaking the fact! If anyone says the Messiah is here or there, we only have to ask ourselves, why the secrecy? When Jesus really comes there will not be silence and secrecy, everybody will know. We must watch, stay spiritually awake be prepared, be expectant and we need to be careful not to be fooled. If anyone's belief does not line up with the words of Jesus regarding His second coming, then they may need to change their theology, because what Jesus said is the absolute truth and it applies to everybody on earth. Jesus must remain in heaven until the perfect day of His return comes around (Acts 3:21). While on earth Jesus may not have known when He was going to return, but He certainly would know now.

In this age of a severe lack of God fearing people, of evolution, false religions, 'feel-good' psychology, rampant homosexuality, pornography, pedophilia and other sexual sins, those who do believe in God and who walk according to His holy ways, need to be beacons of light in this increasingly dark world, regardless of the personal cost to us. Yes, there are many thousands of people coming to know the Lord in a deep and powerful way all over the world, but at the very same time, there is a great falling away from decent morality, good life ethics and true faith in God. Many Christians are becoming carnally minded and tolerate sin like never before; sins like having a homosexual minister, for example. Churches are 'dying' all over the place and although many continue to function, their congregations are spiritually weak, it is amazing to know that most of our so called men of God are teaching false doctrines which does not agree with scripture for example "homosexuality is not a Sin" other include "once you are born again, any sin you commit does not count against you as a believer", brethren in Christ, how on earth will you believe such doctrine, some even say "the Christian walk is a life of success and prosperity". Dear friends in Christ, watch out and be wise with the kind of churches you attend, before it become late! I once had some few minutes of interactions with Mr. John Pepper of JAARS and a pastor in the USA, who visited Tamale with his son Caleb Pepper, in our discussion I asked him of the state of Christianity in America and he told me how Christianity have gone down in America and how most of the churches have closed down and turned into shops. This is really terrible; there is a simultaneous apostasy and revival happening in various places around the world.

Everything is changing, both on the earth and among humanity; weather patterns, earthquakes, tidal surges, storms, strange phenomena in the sky, animals behaving differently than normal, family values, finances, church services, crime, levels of anger and inexplicable rage, and many other weird things taking place everywhere. As genuine believers, how can we cope with the extreme changes? How should we live our lives to shine for God? How can we endure as we await the return of Jesus? The Bible gives us many clues and we will touch on a few of God's commands. We can do nothing about the earth's changes. We can only control how we behave. We need to live righteously, spend time fellowshipping with God in prayer, fellowship with other believers, praise God in song and have a thankful attitude, and serve God as we look to the return of Jesus. *'The grace of God that brings salvation has appeared to all mankind, teaching us to deny ungodliness and worldly desires, we should live soberly, righteously and Godly in the present age. Looking for the blessed hope and glorious appearing of our great God and Savior, the Lord Jesus our Messiah, Who gave Himself to us so He might redeem us from every lawless deed and purify for Himself His own special people zealous for good works'* (Titus 2:11 to 14). Notice in the above verse, the grace of God teaches us to act graciously towards others.

We need to serve God in obedience, led by the Holy Spirit so our good works can endure the test of Judgment Day. *'Every believer's work will be revealed. The Day of Judgment will declare it because it will be revealed in fire and the fire itself will test what sort of work each person's work is. If anyone's work remains, they will receive a reward. If anyone's work is burned, they will suffer loss but they will be saved but only as through fire'* (1 Corinthians 3:13 to 15)

We need to openly demonstrate the Holy Spirit and power of God. *'These signs will follow all those who believe. In My (Jesus') name they will cast out demons, they will speak with new tongues, if they are bitten by snakes or if they drink any deadly thing, it will in no way harm them, they will lay hands on the sick and they will recover'* (Mark 16:17 & 18). *'Our speech and preaching are not in persuasive words of human wisdom, but in demonstration of the Holy Spirit and of power so your faith does not stand in the wisdom of men but in the power of God'* (1 Corinthians 2:4). *'We know we are loved by God and are chosen, and the Gospel came to us, not in word only, but also in power and in the Holy Spirit'* (1 Thessalonians 1:4 & 5).

We must resist temptation to sin and stand against peer pressure. *'My son, if sinners entice you, do not consent ... My son; do not walk in the way with them. Keep your foot from their path for their feet run to evil'* (Proverbs 1:10, 15 & 16). *'Let those who think they stand be careful they do not fall (into sin). No temptation (to sin) has come to you except what is common to man-*

135

kind. God is faithful. He will not allow you to be tempted (to sin) above what you are able to escape so you may be able to endure. Therefore my beloved, flee from idolatry' (1 Corinthians 10:12 to 14). The Bible says twelve times we need to stay sober. *'Watch carefully how you walk, not as unwise people but as wise, redeeming the time because the days are evil. Do not be foolish but understand what the will of the Lord is. Do not be drunk with wine because that is iniquity but be filled with the Holy Spirit, speaking to one another in psalms, hymns and spiritual songs, singing praises in your heart to the Lord, giving thanks always concerning all things in the name of our Lord Jesus, to God the Father'* (Ephesians 5:15 to 20). If Christians think is it okay to drink alcohol they need to rethink their stance. Jesus said, *"If a servant (a Christian) says in their heart, 'My Lord delays His coming,' and begins to beat the servants (become aggressive) and to eat and drink and to be drunken, then the Lord of that servant (Christian) will come in a day when they are not expecting Him and in an hour they do not know and will cut them in two and place their portion (their judgment) with the unfaith-*

136

ful. That servant who knew the Lord's will and did not prepare, nor do what God wanted, will be beaten with many stripes (will be judged severely)'" (Luke 12:45 to 47). If people are secret drinkers, God knows about the secret sin even if people do not.

Remember, we are told to deny ourselves and flee from worldly desires, and drinking booze in secret is not denying oneself. Drinking wine even at a meal can cause a reformed alcoholic to stumble and fall back into their old habit and fall out of the Kingdom of God and in that case, their blood will be on the head of the drinker. If we make a young Christian stumble there is harsh judgment so it is better to refrain from drinking than be judged for causing a young Christian to fall away from God. Temptations will come to all of us but woe to the person who tempts us to sin (Matthew 18:7). Jesus warned, *"Whoever causes one of these little ones who believe in Me to stumble, it would be better for them if a huge millstone was hung around their neck and they were sunk in the depths of the sea"* (Matthew 18:6; Mark 9:42; Luke 17:2). True disciples need to be shining beacons for God and the moderate drinking of wine may not in itself be a sin but for God's light to really shine, it is better to be a good witness and refuse alcohol, even if we are mocked. We must never give in to peer pressure.

When people reject the truth of the Bible, God Himself sends them a delusion. *'The mystery of lawlessness already works in the world ... with all deception of wickedness for those who are lost, because they did not receive the love of the Truth so they might be saved. Because of this, God sends them a strong delusion so they will believe a lie'* (2 Thessalonians 2:7, 10 & 11). We all need to guard ourselves against deception and false religions. *'The Holy Spirit says expressly, in later times (this age we live in) some will fall away from the faith, paying attention to (evil) seducing spirits and doctrines of demons'* (1 Timothy 4:1). The only protection against deception is the love of the Truth and being wary. We need to test their spirit. *'Test all things and hold firmly to what is true'* (1 Thessalonians 5:21). If we encounter a religious person, no matter how genuine they may be, if their teaching does not agree with the scriptures and also does not bring the peace of God we must back away. **'The peace of God which surpasses all understanding will guard your hearts and your minds in Jesus'** (Philippians 4:7). Leaders of false religions have turned the freedom of belief in Jesus to a legalistic, empty, dead religion who deny Jesus is Lord, our Savior and our Messiah. *'There are certain men who crept in (to the church) secretly, those who were long ago written about for this condemnation, ungodly men turning the grace of our God into lasciviousness and denying our only Master, God and Lord, Jesus our Messiah'* (Jude 1:4). *'If you will confess with your mouth Jesus is Lord, and believe in your heart God raised Him from the dead, you will be saved'* (Romans 10:9). *'Do not allow your minds to be corrupted from the simplicity that is in Jesus. Do not accept it if someone comes and preaches another Jesus, or a different spirit, or a different Gospel'* (2Corinthians 11:3 & 4). Examples of such false religions are Mormons who have a so-called Mormon Jesus, and Islam who refer to Jesus as 'Isa' and believe He was a mere human prophet, not the incarnate Son of God Who was sacrificed for our sin.

We must be holy and live holy lives. The appeal to holiness is directly connected with Jesus' coming. To produce holiness in God's people, we need to focus on the coming of the Lord and not things that are happening around us. If we search the scriptures we see there is frequently a call for holiness in God's people and it is based on the reality of His second coming. If we do not frequently declare, proclaim, teach and announce His coming, the standards of holiness in the Body will be below what it should be according to the scriptures. *'Just as He who called you is holy, you yourselves must also be holy in all of your behavior because it is written, "You will be holy for I AM holy'* (1 Peter 1:15 & 16).

We must be blameless, conducting our lives so we are worthy to be called a child of God. We need to be beacons or lights in this dark world. That word 'blameless' is written many times so to be ready for the Day of His second coming, we must be blameless. **'Be blameless in the Day of our Lord Jesus'** (1Corinthians 1:8).

140

'See that you become blameless and harmless, children of God without blemish in the midst of a crooked and perverse generation, among whom you are seen as lights in the world' (Philippians 2:15). *'Jesus has reconciled in the body of His flesh through death, to present you holy and without blemish and blameless before God'* (Colossians 1:22). *'You are witnesses with God, how holy, righteously and blamelessly we behaved ourselves toward you who believe ... Jesus will establish your hearts blameless in holiness before our God and Father at the coming of our Lord Jesus with His saints ... May the God of peace Himself sanctify you completely. May your whole spirit, soul and body be preserved blameless at the coming of our Lord Jesus'* (1 Thessalonians 2:10; 3:13; 5:23). *'Fight the good fight of faith. Lay hold of the eternal life to which you were called ... I command you before God Who gives life to all things and before Jesus ... keep the commandment without spot, blameless, until the appearing of our Lord Jesus, which in the right time He will show up, Who is the blessed and only Ruler, the King of kings and Lord of lords'* (1Timothy 6:12 to 14).

'Be diligent to be found in peace, without blemish and blameless in His sight' (2 Peter 3:14). We need to be eagerly waiting for the coming of the Lord and the first resurrection, and not be complacent.

'Jesus, having been offered once to bear the sins of many will appear a second time, not to atone for sin, but to those who are eagerly waiting for Him for salvation' (Hebrews 9:28). *'Be found in Jesus, not being self-righteous but righteous through faith in Jesus, the righteousness from God by faith so we may know Him and the power of His resurrection and the fellowship of His sufferings, becoming conformed to His death, if by any means we may attain to the resurrection from the dead' (Philippians 3:9 to 11). 'What kind of people ought you to be in holy living and godliness, looking for and earnestly desiring, hastening the coming of the Day of God?'* (2 Peter 3:11 & 12).

We must continue to preach the Gospel no matter how much we are persecuted or treated like dirt. Jesus warned us we would be persecuted because

He was persecuted, but He also said we would receive great rewards in heaven if we endure persecution. *'If they persecuted me they will also persecute you'* (John15:20). *'Blessed are those who are persecuted for righteousness' sake, for theirs is the Kingdom of Heaven. Blessed are you when people reproach you, persecute you and say all kinds of evil against you falsely for my sake. Rejoice and be exceedingly glad for great is your reward in heaven, for that is how they persecuted the prophets who were before you'* (Matthew 5:10 to 12). *'We toil, working with our own hands. When people curse us we bless them. Being persecuted, we endure. Being defamed, we entreat. We are made as the filth of the world, the dirt wiped off by all'* (1 Corinthians 4:12). *'I command you before God and the Lord Jesus, Who will judge the living and the dead at His appearing and His Kingdom, preach the word, be urgent in season and out of season, reprove, rebuke and exhort, with all patience and teaching, for the time will come when they will not listen to sound doctrine, but having itching ears will head up for themselves teachers after their own desires and will turn away their ears from the Truth and turn aside to fables (like evolution, false religions etc.). Be sensible in all things, suffer hardship, do the work of an evangelist and fulfill your ministry ... I (Paul) have fought the good fight. I have finished the course. I have kept the faith. There is stored up for me the crown of righteousness which the Lord, the Righteous Judge will give to me on that day, and not to me only but to all those who have loved his appearing'* (2 Timothy 4:1 to 8). Jesus will not come until the full Gospel of the Kingdom has been preached worldwide in this generation. Not a watered down Gospel, but the Gospel of Jesus. *'This Gospel of the Kingdom will be preached throughout the whole world for a testimony to all the nations and then the end will come'* (Matthew 24:14). When will the end come? When the full Gospel of the Kingdom and Jesus has been preached to all nations

It is the responsibility of all believers. Jesus will not come until the last of the Gentiles have come into the Kingdom of God. *'When the full number of the Gentiles has come in (to the Kingdom) then all Israel will be saved'* (Romans 11:25 & 26). When the day of Jesus' return comes, every sinful thing we have ever done or said that is not confessed and forgiven – anything we are ashamed of will be revealed to all. The only sin God forgives are those we confess to Him. If we do not confess our sins then we are not forgiven. God strongly desires us to take responsibility for our behavior and confessing our sin is accepting responsibility for what we do and say. *'If we confess our sins, God is faithful and righteous to forgive us the sins and to cleanse us from all unrighteousness'* (1 John 1:9). Every single secret thing and every concealed motive will be brought out in to the Light. To avoid that shame and humiliation, our sin needs to be dealt with now by confessing our sin to God, repenting, humbling ourselves before God and asking forgiveness to allow the Holy Spirit to change our innermost heart. *'God will search this out for He knows the secrets of the heart' (Psalm 44:21). 'You (God) have set our iniquities before you, our secret sins in the light of your presence'* (Psalm 90:8). *'There is nothing covered that will not be revealed, and nothing hidden that will not be made known'* (Matthew 10:26).

'Nothing is hidden that will not be revealed, nor anything secret that will not be made known and come to light' (Luke 8:17). To help us endure until Jesus comes again, we need to be constantly reminded of the first coming of Jesus to Israel, His ministry and life that ended with His death on the cross, proclaiming and remembering His sacrifice, and the second coming of Jesus to Jerusalem from where He will rule the whole world with a very strong hand the Bible calls a **'rod of iron'** (Revelation 2:27; 12:5; 19:15). When we share the Gospel, we need to speak directly about the cross and blood of Jesus and not minimize His suffering. All humanity needs to know about Jesus and the results of the cross. We need to remember His sacrifice. Jesus said, *"As often as you eat this bread and drink this cup, you proclaim the Lord's death until He comes'* (1 Corinthians 11:26). It is a privilege to be able to proclaim the Lord's death. When we accept Jesus' sacrifice on the cross, are forgiven and partake of the Lord's Supper, we have no sinful past for all our sin is blotted out. Knowing we will be partakers in the First Resurrection is enough to keep us going when life gets tough. We need to re-

mind ourselves continually of the cross and the return of Jesus and the way to do this is by taking the bread and cup of blessing. When Jesus comes He will come in power and in great glory (Matthew 24:30) to establish His Kingdom on earth.

We need to grow up in God if we are going to be strong enough to endure. *'Jesus appointed apostles, prophets, evangelists, shepherds and teachers for the perfecting of the saints to the work of serving, to build up of the Body of believers in the Messiah until we all attain to the unity of the faith, of the knowledge of the Son of God, to a mature believer, to the measure of the stature of the fullness of Jesus so we may no longer be spiritual children, tossed back and forth and carried about with every wind of doctrine ... but speaking truth in love, we may grow up in all things into Jesus Who is the Head'* (Ephesians 4:11 to 15). The clues mentioned in this Bible study are by no means all we have to do to prepare ourselves for the return of Jesus but it is a start. Life on earth will become harder in every way and when we are strong enough to look up to God and not across to our circumstances, we will know our hearts are ready. Jesus said, *"There will be signs in the sky and the earth will suffer anxiety of nations, perplexed for the roaring of the sea and the waves. People will faint for fear and for expectation of the things coming on the world. The (spiritual) powers of the heavens will be shaken ... When these things begin to happen, look up and lift up your heads because your redemption draws near"* (Luke 21:25 to 28).

Who can endure the day of His coming? Who will stand when He appears? All those who meet God's conditions, who walk in the shadow of the Almighty, who obey all His commands, who fight the good fight, who run the whole race, who keep the faith, who endure to the end, who eagerly await His return. *"Yes, I come quickly."* Amen! Yes, come Lord Jesus (Revelation 22:20).

Amen and God bless you as you help prepare the masses who will endure prior to his second coming. God help us...Amen.

148

Chapter Fourteen

A WORD OF ENCOURAGEMENT TO YOU

As I try to bring this book to a close, my heart is intense. I can only think of the souls that could be reached if the church is awakened, and a new passion and burden is lit like fire shut up in our bones!

There are over 6.5 billion souls alive today on earth! We have a great job ahead of us as a church. We can make a difference. Over 2,000 years ago, the Apostles turned all of Asia upside down with the Gospel with just a few numbers of Christians. What could we do with millions of Apostolic, Holy Ghost-filled believers we have today, if we set our priorities to reach this world?

We will never reach the multitudes from inside of our buildings or comfort zones. We will never reach them by only living a separate and holy lifestyle. If we are to reach them, it will be the biblical way of going into the highways and byways and compelling and persuading them to come in! Luke 14:23.

I want you to think of something for just a minute. I want you to close your eyes for a few seconds and get a clear picture of the most loved person in your life. Once you have that picture, open your eyes and read this next paragraph.

As you are going home, you arrived at your house only to see your house on fire. As you look up, you can see the loved one that you just had a picture of in your mind in the burning house. That loved one is standing in the window screaming for a help out, there are burning flames all around and there is very little time to act quick. When you draw closer to the house, what would you personally do to bring your loved one to safety? Would you risk your life? Would you care who was watching you? Would you do anything you could to bring him or her to safety? Of course you would! You wouldn't stop until him or her is been rescued! Now, let's change the story. Let's say your loved one is in the burning house, and he or she is only having a few moments to live. Him or her is screaming and crying for help, fire is all around; smoke is choking him or her, and is facing death if not rescued. A fire service truck pulls up outside of your burning house. On the truck are the tools to bring your loved one to safety without any serious effort. There is a hosepipe to put out the flame, a ladder to climb up and bring your loved one to safety, an axe to break down the door; everything is in the truck for a successful rescue. Something strange suddenly happened. The fire service man stays in the truck. He is asking himself, *"should I risk injury to go save that person? I wonder it's too dangerous"*. He then thinks; *"well, maybe I should go back to the firehouse and get more training on saving people before I try this"*.

Or maybe he sees a **"no soliciting"** sign or a **"no trespassing"** sign and wonders if he should avoid going up to the house for fear of getting yelled at or maybe consumed by the fire. Maybe he looks at the person in danger and thinks he would be bothering him or her, they would make fun of his uniform, or they might not really want to be saved. So instead of getting out of the truck to easily bring your loved one to safety, he drives away and heads to the closest restaurant to fellowship with the other fire service men. He leaves your loved one to die in the flames. What would you want to do to those fire service personnel if he let your loved one die? What do you think the world should want to do to us when each week, we head to the spiritual firehouses to get more training while passing by hundreds of people facing eternity in hell? What do you think the world thinks of us as we pass them by, ignoring every soul around us to get to the restaurant for fellowship? I realize this is a very hard thing to think about, but how true is this? What about the lost souls? When was the last time you personally won a soul? Have we allowed the cares of life to harden our hearts towards the lost souls of this world?

Everyone I talk to says they love souls and they want to win souls; however, many of them never even try. Have we been deceived? Look around your church. How many new souls are there that you personally brought in? Then look around your city. Find out the population of your city and think about how many souls will face hell if someone doesn't get a burden and go and reach them. You can win souls! You can change your town! You need to do whatever you have to do to realize this and wake up before it's too late! It will be worth the cost! Go on a fast, pray until you weep over the souls of your country, and lay aside everything that gets in the way of outreach and soul winning. It's not God's will that any soul should perish; he has paid a price for their soul. Would you reach them? I pray this book will allow your soul to be stirred. Please do not resist the Holy Ghost. God is trying to use you to reach others! I cannot visualize how any person with the Holy Ghost can possibly be comfortable in letting souls go to hell day after day without taking out your spiritual tools to help rescue them! GO! Go with passion and love. Rescue eve-

ry soul, pulling them out from the lake of fire!
Amen,

As you have read this book, I want you to be
very serious in winning souls for the kingdom of
God, be very passionate, and also develop passion for this lost souls and I want this book to in-
spire you as much as necessary to win the lost at
all cost, souls are very precious to God to the
point that when even one gets converted the entire heavens rejoices. My brethren in the lord,
have souls at heart, you need to develop the spirit of passion and compassion for these lost souls
out there and as you become passionate about
these lost souls, you will be hard-pressed to witness the salvation of God to them, rise up today
and win the lost souls around you and as you do
that God will grow in your heart compassion and
passion. Be enthused to win the lost at all cost;

**"... Compel them to come in that my house may
be filled"** Luke 14:23.

These words always keep buzzing in my spirit:

"that my house maybe filled"! "That my house may be filled"!! Dear readers, never forget that there is still more room at the cross for one more soul to be saved. Rise up and go and compel them to come and serve the living God. Evangelism is not intended to be done in a vacuum, it should be related to church expansion, all our hard work to lead people to the Lord, must bear fruits. We must see our efforts filling our church buildings. And whatever be the case a pastor must see that, there is still room at the cross for one more soul and I strongly believe that if we have this in mind, God will use us to fill the church. A pastor must never be satisfied with the size of his congregation and we must let these things motivate as to win the lost souls for God. May the Spirit of God rest upon you, one and all, for Jesus Christ's sake! Amen.

20 TIPS TO BECOME ACTIVE IN SOUL WINNING

1. Get past your excuses- the world needs preachers, your pastor can't be everywhere

2. Get past your fears – you may lose some friends, family, neighbors but gain souls

3. Schedule Soul Winning Times – force yourself to do it, joy is an evangelistic force

4. Rebound – go back at it after getting many "NOs"

5. Be soul conscious – Be more concerned about keeping people from hell than your personal things

6. Appearance – smile, glow, be presentable, be happy

7. The Two Principle – Jesus always sent out in pairs, for relationship, communication, reinforces the message

8. Keep the Bible close at hand – prepare 5-10 easy-to-remember scriptures about salvation

9. Be filled with the Holy Spirit – pray in tongues before you go out, stir up your gift first

10 1 Thessalonians 1:5 – be fully persuaded about what you are saying, Kingdom is word AND power, go believing for results, have an easy answer to 'why am I here Lord?'

11. Be Kind – don't get frustrated, don't quarrel, be open to manifest the love of God

12. Create a home for acceptance – look for God in others: crosses, tattoos, symbols are open doors already you can build on, these people are already looking

13. Be a good listener – don't steam roll over people with the gospel, God Loves you, He has a plan for your life, can I pray for you

14. Stay on topic – the Gospel is the focus, don't be too busy for God's work, BUSY=**Believers Under Satan's Yoke**, Eph 5:16 opportunity, Col 4:5 redeem the time, people are Running to and fro in the earth, now is the time, are you Spirit driven or flesh driven? Acts 1:2 = Go

15. Ask Truth Questions: point out the need for a savior, have you ever lied, stolen, lusted, that's sin, Romans 5:8 says people are lost, that's the reason Jesus came to die, He is the way, Romans 3:23 all guilty

16. Be Simple – short trips, don't overload people with the Bible

17. The Goodness of God leads men to repentance – Romans 2:4, Romans 6:23 the wages of sin are death

18. Stay in the presence of God – be at peace, not anxious, this is this life of a believer, enjoy His grace

19. Be a model of faith – let people see how good God has been in your life, share your testimonies

20. Look for diamonds in the rough – many don't know that God is looking for them wherever they are.

"The fruit of the righteous is a tree of life; and he that winneth souls is wise" - Proverbs 11:30

BIBLIOGRAPHIES

1. *Bible House:* **1976, Holy Bible, Authorize King James Version. North Carolina: C.D. Stampley enterprise, Inc.**

2. **The New Scofield Reference Bible with Concordance, New York**

3. **They All Went to Hell,** *Evangelist Dag Heward-Mills*

4. *Rev. Park* Yong Gyu**, Divine Revelation, South Korea,** *www.divinerevelation.info/* **PARK**

5. **Evangelism By Fire,** *Evangelist Reinard Bonke*

6. **The case for Easter,** Lee Strobel

Made in the USA
Lexington, KY
16 July 2017